Honeymoon in Baghdad

Honeymoon in Baghdad

HEIDI
RADKIEWICZ

ISBN Paperback: 978-1-947368-75-0
ISBN eBook: 978-1-947368-76-7
LCN: 2018934050

I dedicate this book to:

1. God—none of this would have happened without you. Thanks for having my back. Best battle buddy, ever.

2. The love of my life, my best friend, my battle buddy, my soul mate . . . my everything. You and I are in this for the long haul, and I couldn't imagine anyone else standing beside me to take on this crazy but awesome life of ours.

3. Wyatt and Summer—you guys mean the world to your father and me. We would do anything for you two, and I mean anything.

4. My dad, mom, stepmom, and stepdad, for raising me the way you did (I know you didn't raise me to use profanity, so disregard the swearing in this book), showing me how to love, giving me unconditional support, and helping shape who I am today.

5. My sister, aka "Donny"—you are my best friend, my twin separated at birth by five years. Thank you for always supporting me and being there for me. We have an inseparable bond.

6. My in-laws—it was a rough start, but you've been so supportive of us and helped us in so many ways that I don't think of you as "in-laws" anymore, just "mom and dad."

7. Every member of the US military—past, present, and future.

8. The United States of America—the greatest country on God's green earth.

Growing Up

"How about that one?"

"A million billion miles," she said. "Beyond everything."

"Think we'll ever make it there?" From the direction of the house, I heard my mom whistling for the dogs.

We were lying out in the field behind my mom's farmhouse, the night sky bright with stars overhead. Grass tickled the backs of my legs, and you could practically feel the hum of the insects as their chorus filled my ears. My sister Heather and I were pointing at the blindingly bright pinpricks of the Milky Way and trying to guess how far from us they were. She was five years older than me, and it felt like she knew everything there was to know.

She shook her head. "It's too far to go alone."

"Yeah, but, maybe, if I've got a good friend . . . I think I can get pretty far," I said, with the unthinking confidence of a seven-year-old. "There's lots to see."

In the years since that quiet night, I have never made it to the stars, but I have found a good friend. Together, we've traveled the world, and we've had our fair share of adventures. I'm always surprised by how hard it is to take those first few steps out the door, but we still take them. There's lots to see, after all.

* * *

July 2003, Baghdad, Iraq. My face is plastered to the window of my 915 semi-truck, taking in the mayhem around us. The smell of burning tires comes in waves as we drive past smoldering wreck after smoldering wreck. The convoy creeps slowly by, and my truck nears a cluster of locals, shouting and arguing and pointing at . . . a headless body in the road, next to a car that until very recently had not been a convertible. The top has been sheared clean off, nothing from the dashboard up. Infantry pick their way through the mess, until finally a gap in the activity reveals a dingy white robe, a single sandal, filthy hands pointing straight up at the sky, fingers curled as if around a steering wheel. Ten and two.

And blood pooling around him.

I grew up in a small town in northern Iowa called Eagle Grove, surrounded by tranquil, rolling fields of corn and soybeans. In the summer, the sun beats down like a hammer, and in the humidity, the buzzing of bugs is constant, matched only by the earthy aroma of the local granary and the neighboring pig and cattle farms. Autumn brings the harvest, heralded by the rumble of combines and the shock of color in the trees. Winters are harsh, with bone-chilling temperatures that dip below freezing and a wind that cuts through even the heaviest of coats. And every year, spring feels like a miracle. The town was small—no more than a thousand families, most of them the descendants of German or Norwegian settlers, their politics mostly conservative, their religion mostly Christian. They were good people, and to us, the town felt safe. It was the sort of place where life moved gently, where you kept one eye always on the sky.

My best friends and I would swim at our local town pool in an effort to escape the heat and humidity of the scorching Iowa summers. One day, Jen, Tiff, and I all dove under the water at the same time to see how long we could hold our breath. We came back up to the surface to find that we were the only ones in the pool—everyone else was screaming and running toward the exit. That was when I saw it. Dark greenish clouds rolling up fast, a funnel forming just over the cornfield in the distance.

"Tornado!" I shouted, grabbing in the water for my friends. "Let's get out of here!" We jumped out of the pool and ran to the fence, but when we got there, where could we go? Our parents had dropped us off, and home was on the other side of town. Frantic, my eye fell on a woman and her daughter getting into their car and pulling my friends with me, I asked if we could get in too. We didn't know the woman well, but no one was a true stranger in this town. Without hesitation, she opened the door and we all piled in. Together, we went to the closest house she knew of and took shelter from the storm. When the tornado had passed, she took us home. That was what life in Eagle Grove was like. You might not know everyone very well, but when it came down to it, you knew that you could trust people.

* * *

Debris had closed off several lanes of traffic, slowing our convoy's progress to a crawl. Shabby tan houses on either side. Angry pedestrians shuffling in and out of traffic. Any one of them could have a bomb. Any one of the houses could be hiding a sniper. But my mind's eye kept drifting back to the man in the road. To the head he was missing. He'd been driving—that much was clear—and given the state of his car, he'd surely had a bomb. He must have been trying to hit a convoy. He must have misjudged something, the speed or the distance, and instead of hitting the cab and detonating the bomb, he'd slid under the trailer, moving at speeds fast enough to take off the top of his car. Along with his head.

SGT Koster in the driver's seat glanced over at me. "You see that dude?" he asked.

I turned to him. Held his gaze. Neither of us could believe what we were seeing. "I wish I hadn't," I said. "That's jacked up."

As the words came out of my mouth, I saw a strange smile bloom on Koster's face, and I felt the tension of the moment drain out of me. I started to giggle, and couldn't stop. Soon Koster was laughing with me. We didn't understand it. There was nothing funny here. But we'd been attacked so often lately that the sight of that pathetic, incompetent insurgent, his hands still ready for the road, felt more like a relief than a horror.

* * *

In Eagle Grove, life was simple and uncomplicated, and that's how I liked it. I spent a lot of my evenings home with my parents—not because they kept me in, but because apart from basketball and football games, there wasn't much to do outside of the house, and kids tended to make their own fun.

After school, my sister and I, sometimes accompanied by our stepbrothers, would jump up on the farm's bean buggy—an overgrown Erector Set–looking piece of farming equipment designed to ride over the tops of soybean plants, clocking in at a *whopping* eight miles per hour—and tool around the farm, pretending we were in the Indianapolis 500. On a farm, you need imagination and the willingness to take your fun wherever you find it.

That ethos went for town life too. Some of the fun was safe and innocent—but some of it wasn't. Most kids experimented with alcohol and sex long before I was ready even to think about taking those kinds of risks. Admittedly, I'd bloomed late. My parents were never explicit about the way men and women fit together, either because of their own natural shyness about the subject, or because they each expected the other to be responsible for "The Talk." It wasn't until high school that I had a full appreciation for the truth about the stork, and I hated the idea of putting anything in my body that could change who I was. I wouldn't risk an STD or pregnancy just to stave off a little boredom, but more importantly, everything I had been taught told me to wait. Just the idea of sex scared me.

But I don't want to suggest that my life was boring, because it certainly was not. Once we could drive, my friends and I spent our Friday nights cruising up and down the main street, waving and shouting at our classmates in the other cars, relishing the sheer joy of being young and mobile and free. With "Glycerine" by Bush playing on the radio, we might even be a little adventurous, and cruise out to a neighboring town, someplace where we hadn't known every other boy since preschool. Through the car windows, we'd lock eyes with these new, exotic boys and we'd smile and blush. It seems painfully innocent now, but at the time, it felt bold and thrilling.

One by one, my friends hooked up with steady boyfriends, but I never did. I guessed that boys were ignoring me because I never had much in the way of curves—I've always been slender and active, and puberty didn't change much about my frame. But their inattention never really bothered me. There were 250 students in my entire high school, and I'd grown up with all of them. The idea of dating within that pool had about as much appeal as dating one of my stepbrothers.

When my senior year drew to a close, I decided to look for a summer job outside of corn country, for once. My dad and stepmom had taken us on a family vacation to Yellowstone a few years back, and I'd loved the hot springs, the geysers, and the bison that roamed free throughout the park. I'd been obsessed with grey wolves since I was little, and I'd heard that the park was supporting a grey wolf population boom. It wasn't even a question—when I saw that Old Faithful Lodge was hiring, I jumped at the chance.

Despite my enthusiasm, it was easy to be nervous. The job itself wasn't amazing—what food court summer job would be?—but more importantly, I'd never really been away from home before. Sure, there was that time at church camp, but that didn't count because I was so unhappy that I convinced my dad to come pick me up after two days. No matter. I wouldn't let my inexperience stop me. I packed my bags, and both sets of my parents drove me to the Minneapolis airport.

By the end of the ride, I was a wreck. I'd never flown before, and visions of the plane fire-balling out of the blue played endlessly behind my closed eyes. But it was too late to back down. We said our tearful goodbyes, and I got onto the plane. I mostly managed to keep calm, right until I got to my seat. An older man had the seat next to me, and as I sat down, something about his expression punctured the little composure I had left. I burst into tears. All the fear of flying, of maybe never seeing my family again, of going far away from everything I'd known—it all poured out of me. I don't know what this kind old man thought of being seated next to a wailing teenager, but I thank God that he was there. He asked what was wrong, and then proceeded to talk me through the entire flight. He described every part of the plane and how it functioned. He showed me all the safety measures in place. He told me bizarrely comforting statistics about the relative safety of air travel. And he distracted me from the feeling in the pit of my chest—the growing distance between myself and everyone I'd ever loved. In the end, the flight was beautiful, and I got to Yellowstone feeling whole and ready.

That feeling didn't last. When I was working, I was okay—my teammates were fun, and we were exposed to busloads of people from all over the world. But while working kept my mind and body busy, the homesickness roared back into place when I wasn't working. My dorm mate, a sweet girl from Georgia, was very social, so she'd somehow built her own group of new friends within a couple of days of our arrival. I'd never had to make new friends before, and I've never been outgoing, so while she was gone a lot, I was alone in the dorm. It was miserable.

No amount of walking around Old Faithful or hanging out with bison could make up for that crushing loneliness.

I made it two weeks before crying "uncle" and calling my parents. They put up a fight—they knew that I should finish out the job—but in the end, every parent caves at the cries of their baby girl. I came home. At least I'd lasted longer than at church camp.

I spent the rest of the summer with my friends and family, reveling in the familiar comforts and haunts, trying not to read too much into the homesickness that had lost me Yellowstone. I was planning to go to junior college in the fall, and my parents were sure that I wasn't ready. I have to admit, after the Yellowstone experience, even I began to have doubts. Maybe I was just incapable of living away from home. Maybe I'd be stuck in Eagle Grove for the rest of time, forever a kid in my parents' homes, never living my own life.

I don't know if that was the thought that put me over the edge, or the fact that my best friends were leaving home, too, but when the time came to pack up and head out, I knew I was ready.

It helped that the campus was only an hour's drive away. Home was there if I needed it, and just the idea that I *could* go home if I wanted to was enough to keep me from needing to make that trip. All I needed was to keep myself busy.

I took multiple jobs, but the one at FedEx Ground was my favorite. I set up my schedule so that work started directly after my classes, meaning that even if I wanted to, I had no time to feel lonely. But it was more than that. The friends I made at work were the ones who introduced me to whole new ideas and perspectives. One of these friends was even responsible for giving me a Nine Inch Nails CD—basically introducing me to heavy metal—music that, to this day, makes me feel rebellious and strong.

I'd always been the sweet, obedient girl next door, but the music brought out something previously unknown in me. At FedEx, my time was filled with unloading packages from trucks and then loading those same packages onto different trucks. It doesn't sound like the sort of job that would keep your mind from tying itself in knots, but there was something soothing about it. The rhythm, possibly, or the way bending and lifting and bending and lifting just wears you out. I'd wake up every morning with that familiar ache that meant my body had done something useful, and every night I'd be asleep before my head hit the pillow. It didn't hurt that I was the only girl doing the job. My male coworkers were impressed that I could haul a ninety-pound package, and they made me feel like one of the team.

The actual class part of college was not as much fun. I spent most of my time working, so much so that I didn't make a lot of time for my studies, and even when I wasn't working, the temptation to be out in the sunshine was always stronger than the pull of a textbook. If I wasn't fishing, I was out roller blading or running. I belong outdoors. School was going to have to be a *lot* more interesting if it wanted to compete with sunshine.

During the weekends, my girlfriends and I would drive out to Cedar Falls to go dancing. Dancing was a chance to let loose, to remind ourselves of who we'd always been together.

Jenny was almost as strait-laced as me, and Tiffany broke all the rules. We'd get out on the floor and it was like the years and the distance vanished in the space of a song. And sometimes, when the song was done, we'd have a little time to get to know a guy or two. I never went beyond talking with them—I had strong ideas about what sort of man I wanted to be with, and these guys did not fit the bill.

I'd always known what the man I would marry would be like. A God-fearing, masculine man who was kind-hearted, generous, level-headed, and loving, with a willingness to do whatever needed to be done. A true partner. I knew that men like that existed. My father was one, after all. I wouldn't settle for anything less.

After two years of middling classroom experience, all I'd really learned was that school was kind of boring. The world seemed like a big place, full of options within options, and I hated feeling like I *had* to do something without knowing what it was.

The one thing I really knew was that I'd be fine doing something physical. I had real muscles, and I knew how to use them. And that was when the lightbulb went on. Both my father and stepdad had been in the Army National Guard. From their stories, I knew what to expect, I knew that my body would be able to handle it, and since it wasn't the regular army, I knew that I could keep the rest of my life on track. And it turned out that if I signed up, the army would promise to pay for the rest of my education as soon as I figured out what that meant.

Two years earlier, I couldn't have committed to a summer of watching grey wolves and bison frolic in a national park, but when the recruiter handed me a pen, I signed on the dotted line. I devoted six years of my life to Uncle Sam.

My family and friends couldn't believe that I'd signed myself up. Little Miss Heidi joined the army? Who was this girl?

And I couldn't wait for the adventure.

CHAPTER 1

Bring It

Basic Training. Fort Jackson, South Carolina, October 2000. We knew that basic training had truly begun when, one morning at reception, as a group of us stood in formation, waiting to hear our orders for the day, a bus screeched to a halt next to us. A dozen drill sergeants poured out, shouting and screaming as they ran, "Get your asses in the bus, *now*! Y'all got thirty seconds!" Before that moment, I hadn't even been scolded, let alone screamed at, and as the drill sergeants raced toward me, I couldn't help but think, "What the hell did I get myself into?" I blocked out the world as I ran to the bus, my duffle bag full of army gear thumping against my back, praying that no one would notice me.

I chose a seat toward the back of the bus, all while a drill sergeant was screaming at the recruits: "Sit down! Put your elbows on your knees! Put your heads between your hands, and CLOSE YOUR EYES!"

I obeyed, but I couldn't for the life of me understand why they were so specific about how we sat. It seemed completely unnecessary.

But as the bus started to move, I could hear a drill sergeant screaming at a recruit in front of me, "Did you open your eyes, private? Did I seriously see you open your eyes? Did your momma drop you on your head as a baby? Why can't you follow simple instructions?" All that screaming over someone opening her eyes? This was going to be a very long ten weeks.

* * *

I wished we could look out the windows. If we couldn't see where we were—the reasoning went—we couldn't hack basic training, we wouldn't know which way to go, so we wouldn't be able to run away. As a girl who'd always needed an out, I don't mind telling you that this wasn't the most welcome news. I had to take a minute and remember why I was there: adventure, patriotism, and the bone-deep knowledge that I could *do this*. There was no chance in hell that I would try to run away.

It's a drill sergeant's job to break you down. If you can't deal with someone getting in your face, screaming at you, and working you to death, then basic isn't for you. You wake up at 5:00 a.m. or earlier, don your PT (physical training) gear, make your bed so precisely that a quarter can bounce off the sheets, and head down to formation. After formation, you start your PT for the day. PT consists of a two-mile run (in formation, while singing in cadence), pushups, sit-ups, and other calisthenics.

Once you're done with PT, there's breakfast, but you need your proper uniform for that, so back to the barracks you go. I was always hungry in basic training. Probably from the constant physical exercise, or maybe because I couldn't have food anytime I wanted. After PT one day, I ran upstairs with everyone, salivating at the thought of grits and pancakes, and changed into my uniform extra fast. I sprinted out the door before all the other recruits were even out of their PT gear. I thought maybe I would get to eat first if I got to formation first.

As soon as I rounded the corner out of the barracks, a drill sergeant caught me.

"Private Ehen, I bet you think you're special for being first to formation."

I had discovered the flaw in my plan to eat sooner.

"While we wait for the rest of the company, you can do some front-back-gos."

Front-back-gos consist of: front (pushups), back (sit-ups), go (run in place). You do each one until the drill sergeant calls out the next move, always in that order. I think I did twenty minutes of front-back-gos that morning, which just made me hungrier.

The army wants you to operate as a team, and in a team, there is no first and no last. There's just the team. Sometimes you have to learn the hard way.

After breakfast came regular training. Men and women train together in the army. We do everything together, really. The only things female recruits do separately from male recruits are sleeping and showering, but I'm sure some recruits managed to even do that together.

There were three different phases of training: Red, White, and Blue. Red Phase consisted of field exercises in which the drill sergeants put major emphasis on working together, because teamwork is a big deal. White Phase was spent road marching to the rifle range and rappelling. The last phase, Blue, was serious weapons training.

I loved rappelling. It was unquestionably my favorite part of basic. Hanging in midair, your feet against a hundred-foot wall, ropes draping off you, a giant belt around your waist to keep you from falling to your death . . . It feels precarious and exhilarating and strangely freeing. Once you're there, one hand behind your back and the other guiding the rope, you have to do the opposite of everything your body is telling you to do: You lean back. You jump down to the ground. Every time I landed, I only wanted to do it over again.

The worst part was the gas chamber. Being in a gas chamber with your mask on isn't that bad; you're just breathing clean, filtered air. But the point of the gas chamber isn't apparent until the last minute or two, where they make you take off the masks and experience the reality of CS gas (tear gas). At this point you realize how well your mask truly functioned. Breathing in CS gas felt as though someone had put a noose around my lungs, lit a match, and tossed it down my throat. I was sure that there'd been some terrible mistake and my drill sergeant was actually trying to kill me. When we stumbled out of the gas chamber, every orifice in our bodies was oozing and we were profoundly disoriented. Some recruits even ran into each other. We just wanted the burning to stop.

During Blue Phase, we got to operate the bigger weapons: the SAW (squad automatic weapon), AT-4s, hand grenades, and grenade launchers. I found nothing more exhilarating than having a massive AT-4 sandwiched between my tiny hands and propped up on my shoulder. The first time, the drill sergeant chose me specifically to shoot this beast. I shouted, "Back blast area, all clear!" And BOOM! A giant antitank rocket shot out of the barrel at 950 feet per second, headed toward a target a half-mile away, and when it hit, it was blown to smithereens. Smoke billowed out from the blast, and I discovered that I was still on my feet. Of course, he'd chosen me. He knew the kickback wouldn't knock me to the ground. He wanted to prove to the other recruits that it was nothing to fear.

Blue Phase also involved two very long road marches: a 10K and a 15K. A road march requires you to carry all your gear, easily fifty pounds. Remember, I clocked in at 103 pounds, but I still had to carry my rucksack, my (much too big for my head) Kevlar, a load-bearing equipment jacket on my chest (which held my canteens and magazines), and my M-16 in my hands. Not to mention my fatigues and army boots. They say that an ant can carry its own body weight dozens of times over, and I've got to say, I feel you, brother. After every march, I was certain that my arms and legs were going to spontaneously combust. The exhaustion and feeling of accomplishment were overwhelming. The only thing I wanted was to fall into my bed and sleep for the next fifteen hours.

The end of the Blue Phase was the biggest event for a basic training recruit. Everything came down to one last event, the night infiltration course. This night was filled with climbing and crawling obstacles, and learning to shoot our weapons at night, but the challenge that stood out was the last event of the evening. I had heard rumors, but I was sure it wasn't real until I heard the rounds being fired and I saw the tracers streaking across the field. Live rounds, at head height. We were low-crawling the length of a football field while some lunatic on the other side shot live rounds over our heads. The whole experience is designed to be chaotic, to push you to your limits. As you crawl face down in the dirt, your M-16 in hand, you're essentially crawling through a hurricane of all the things that could raise your anxiety level. Bullets fly overhead. Explosions go off right next to you. Sirens blare disturbing sounds like babies crying, and people screaming in pain, all while drill sergeants scream at you in the dark. There's a constant smell of gunpowder, and burning explosives fill the air. They'll do anything they can think of to break you.

But what was I going to do? This was what I'd signed up for. I got down to the ground, my face planted into the sand, my low-crawl stance pristine, and I took off for the other end. As I made my way, my face covered in dirt and sand, the chill of the ground crept into me, but not once did I lift my head up off the ground to see where I was going. My mission was to make it to the other side while keeping my head attached to my body. And I did. It felt amazing to reach the other side of the field, to stand up, and to realize that I hadn't been shot. I knew the army wouldn't put us in a place where we could really get shot during training, but, with all the psychological games they were playing with the environment, you were never really sure. There was always a little voice in the back of your head telling you that you were in real danger. It wasn't until much later in my military career that the point of this exercise really became clear.

I loved basic training. I mean, I loved the physical part of it, not the screaming and degradation, but in the end, even that stuff didn't bother me. My drill sergeant liked me. I was a hard worker, and I always tried to outdo everyone else. I've always been competitive in that way. And I know that it was all an act. They had to break us down and put us back together the way the army wanted us to be: as soldiers. Basic training was intended to test us physically, but even more important, it was designed to build our mental toughness. Mental toughness is what really counts when you face hardship and danger. The mental challenge of basic training is far more difficult than any of the physical trials.

More than simply finding out that I was a perfect fit for the army, I also learned a lot about my fellow citizens. The people I went to basic training with were from every part of the country, from the East Coast to the West Coast and most places in between. I had known what life was like in a small, rural, midwestern town, where we were all mostly alike, but at basic I met a girl from South Carolina named Bacon. She was loud and opinionated, and we got along together like we had grown up and known each other our whole lives. We had absolutely nothing in common in terms of where and how we grew up, but we were both good people who shared the same morals, values, and patriotism. There was an unspoken loyalty between us that I didn't expect to find in basic. At the end of the day, we are all Americans. That's all that mattered.

We'd all grown stronger and more certain of ourselves. Hell, when I left basic training, I weighed a whopping 118 pounds, and most of that was muscle. Gaining fifteen pounds over ten weeks was a pretty amazing feat, especially considering that in basic training, most people lost that much weight. Some lost even more. I managed to pack on fifteen pounds partially because of the muscle I gained, and partially because the drill sergeants were on a mission to fatten me up. They made sure I finished every meal, and even made me have dessert, which was unheard of in basic. Even better, the drill sergeants didn't want my desserts to separate me from the team, so they started letting a battle buddy get dessert with me. I was a popular battle buddy during mealtime.

After basic, I completed my AIT (Advanced Individual Training), which focuses on a specific job in the army. I'd decided to be a semi-truck driver. I know the picture is a little funny: this tiny, 118-pound blonde chick behind the wheel of an eighteen-wheeler. That was me. There was something about being in a truck that big that made me feel powerful, especially when I was packing an M-16 rifle. I could take on the world.

* * *

I got home, flush with this new sense of my own power and purpose, and discovered that Eagle Grove felt strangely small. I love my parents, and I was never going to disrupt their lives, but I needed something more. Heather was tired of working her butt off in Des Moines and was really, *really* ready for a change, so together, we decided to strike out into the country and build new lives for ourselves. We considered going to Bemidji in Minnesota—we had some family up there and it had all the fishing and camping we could want—but we realized we weren't up for winters that were worse than those we'd grown up with in Iowa. Eventually we settled on

Fort Collins, in Colorado. Heather's boyfriend was in Denver, and she liked the idea of being closer to him. I couldn't really object—Fort Collins had mountains, sunshine, a life outdoors, and, most importantly, it wasn't Iowa. It had everything we wanted. We packed the U-Haul, hitched both our cars to it, and hit the road.

Heather is like me. You spend your whole childhood squabbling with your sister, but none of it matters in the end. You're still working with the same genes, the same upbringing, the same certainty that things are going to turn out okay. We look alike—blonde and slight, with playful faces that make us look like we're only barely refraining from giggling—and we approach life in the same way. Heather never joined the National Guard, but she geared up for taking on the world in her own style. While she was in Des Moines, she'd worked herself to the bone. Her full-time job was at the courthouse, and she used waitressing to fill in the gaps around it. Sometimes she was so tired that she'd fall asleep in the elevator on the way home. She needed this new beginning just as much as I did.

We were supposed to be finishing our degrees. That was the official mission, and sure, I could see how it was the logical, grown-up, responsible thing to do. But while basic training had given me a ton of new skills and amped up my self-confidence, it hadn't given me a sense of what I was supposed to do with my life. As far as I was concerned, the step after basic was to move to Colorado and just *live*. There was nothing attractive about going back to school. *Maybe later*, I told myself.

We rented a two-bedroom apartment a few blocks away from Colorado State University. The place was perfect for two kids just starting out—enough communal space to keep us together, enough privacy to keep us from being in each other's hair. We kept our mountain bikes in the living room. We decorated with neon beer signs we'd found in an antique shop and plastic milk crates to hold up the TV. Our furniture was all hand-me-downs and thrift-store stuff—a rocking chair from grandma, a floral couch from the 1970s, a squishy taco chair that would swallow you if you let it. It wasn't pretty, but we didn't expect to be inside much. Why focus on your interior décor when you've got the Rockies to explore?

We got jobs, and when we weren't working we enjoyed ourselves. The mountain bikes weren't for show—there were mountains that needed biking! We hiked, we ran, and we got out the rollerblades and took over our local park. And, once we felt comfortable with Fort Collins's daytime activities, we thought it might be time to see what happened at night.

We decided to start big, with the trendiest bar in downtown Fort Collins, but when I walked into the bar, I immediately felt like we were different from the other girls there. They were wearing tight, revealing dresses, and we were dressed like we were going to the Iowa state fair. I didn't even own a dress. I hadn't even thought about what we were wearing when we left the apartment. It didn't register that a college club in Fort Collins would be any different from a college club in Iowa.

The clothes weren't the only difference. This place was packed—so crowded that just moving around was a challenge. Scantily dressed girls danced on the bar, and you couldn't move without bumping into some sweaty frat boy. I looked at those girls on the bar, and thought, "What floozies." Who would do that? I'm sure Heather was thinking the same thing, but it was too loud to talk.

We tried to get close to the bar, but with every elbow that rammed into me, my mood was souring. The floor was sticky from drunks spilling their drinks, and cigarette smoke filled the air. We couldn't get to the bar, so we just stopped, standing on the periphery with our arms crossed. This wasn't turning out the way we wanted it to; this was not the way the night should have gone.

"You want to get out of here?" I shouted, hoping Heather would hear me over the crowd.

"Yep," she said. "Let's just go home."

Once we were in the car and on our way back to the apartment, I looked over at Heather, grumbling to herself, and I said, "How was anyone supposed to dance in there?"

"It's almost as if the girls were just there to get drunk and grind on guys."

"Yeah. Those girls on the bar, is that what they call *dancing?*" I said as we pulled into our parking spot. "They looked more like strippers to me."

We got inside, and Heather paced in the kitchen while I sprawled on the couch. A couple of minutes passed as she rattled cupboards and got herself a glass of water until her voice came floating out: "We're going about this the wrong way." She came back out to the living room, a new, harder set to her eyes. "This is our time. We should enjoy ourselves—on our terms."

The next night, we tried a different club, one called The Matrixx. We slapped on some war paint (makeup), donned our best armor (cutoff shorts, a tight T-shirt and tennis shoes), and hit the club. We heard the music blasting (Daft Punk, "One More Time") long before we got inside, so loud that I could feel the rhythm pulsing through my body. The dance floor was a sea of people, encircled by the bar. This was starting to feel like the club from last night, only bigger. I know what you're thinking. *Isn't this how clubs are supposed to be?* To most people, Fort Collins is probably a pretty small town, but for me, it was the largest city I'd ever lived in. I wasn't used to the city college campus vibe. We almost left again, but I saw some stairs leading up to a platform that overlooked the rest of the club. It looked pretty empty. It had potential. We ordered a couple of Long Island iced teas, to help us relax, and considered our next move.

Heather and I don't dance like other people. We have real moves—a style that doesn't rely on hip thrusting or grinding. It needs space. It didn't take long for us to decide to commandeer the upstairs platform for ourselves. We were going to get our crazy on in comfort.

There was no one up there at first, which was definitely a good thing. Our style starts with simple bopping, but it gets crazy pretty quick. Give us enough space and we'll start running and jumping and twirling—generally goofing around, just having a great time. It's the kind of dancing where you can't scare if other people are watching. But they were.

"Heather, everyone is staring at us."

The people below us had looked up, seen how much fun we were having, and now were coming to join us. Dozens of them swarmed up the stairs, until it got so crowded on that little platform that the only place with enough space to dance anymore was back down on the floor.

It was an electric night. I felt like we'd pushed ourselves to be out in the world, to share it with strangers, and it had paid off. Even when it feels uncomfortable and awkward, taking a risk or two can open you up to a life you'd never have expected.

But no matter how diverting the sights and pleasures of Fort Collins were, I knew that I had responsibilities that far surpassed my own whims—and even my educational "mission." Every month, I had to drill with a National Guard unit. Sometimes this meant paperwork, vehicle maintenance, or just keeping my rifle-eye sharp—things you'd expect to do wherever there was an armory—but I was a truck driver, so I had to drill with a transportation unit, and there wasn't one in Fort Collins. So, every month, I ended up having to drive sixty miles north to Laramie, Wyoming, where a construction unit drilled. You'll notice that construction and transportation aren't the same thing, but don't worry. They have enough in common that I could drill with this unit and fulfill my requirements. All the same, sixty miles was a long way, particularly in mountain country. Rather than make that drive four times in one weekend, it made sense for me to bunk at the armory every time I went up.

The two days of drill are usually really busy, but at night, soldiers let loose. Laramie is home to the University of Wyoming, so it has a healthy supply of college bars, and I made sure that I sampled the best of whatever was on offer.

The more I traveled, the better acquainted I became with the character of our country. Where Fort Collins was a mix of city and outdoor living, Laramie was decidedly "country." This was a cowboy town. The bars were smaller and musty and smelled of smoke and stale beer. Instead of big dance halls, the cowboys occupied themselves with darts and pool, and they had an elaborate sort of courtliness that, even after a day under the engine block of an eighteen-wheeler, made me feel delicate. I liked it. And I could always find a dance partner.

But those dance partners never became anything more serious. Not for lack of trying on their part—I was just really hard to impress. Back in Mason City, I once got to know a guy I really enjoyed hanging out with. On a whim, I challenged him to arm wrestle. Unfortunately for him, he couldn't beat me, and I totally lost interest. A guy would look good, but then he'd open his mouth, or prove his lack of masculinity, and ruin the illusion, and I was never willing to stick it out past that moment.

And then . . . I met Jake.

Jake was part of the Laramie unit. Drilling with him was a pleasure; he knew what he was doing and got it done quickly and efficiently. He'd charmed everyone in his unit. And, with an athletic build, some good height, and a bit of scruff, Jake was easy on the eyes.

The only problem I could see was that he was out with a different girl every weekend. Was he a player? Maybe he just had a bunch of female friends? I couldn't tell, and I didn't want to get in the middle of whatever drama he had going on. That is, I *wanted* to—who wouldn't, right?—but my flirting skills left a lot to be desired. Just the thought of approaching him

26

left my knees trembling and heart beating faster than it had during the night infiltration exercise. I had no game. I prepared to spend the rest of my life ogling Jake from a distance.

But then the towers came down, and everything changed.

CHAPTER 2

War and Love

Everyone remembers where they were when the twin towers fell. I was working at FedEx Ground in Fort Collins. My shift had started at 5:00 a.m., and bleary-eyed, I'd watched the day dawn bright and clear. The first I heard of the attack was from one of the drivers, leaning out of his cab to tell me. "Did you hear that a plane crashed into one of the twin towers?" I could hear the shock and confusion in his voice, but it didn't mean anything to me. Yet. I'd never even heard of the twin towers.

It had to be a pilot error. Or mechanical problems. An awful tragedy, but nothing more. At that point, I was still thinking of it like any plane crash—the "into a building" aspect of it hadn't registered. I don't think I'd even considered the possibility that the tower might collapse, let alone the idea that someone had done this on purpose.

When I got home, I found Heather curled up in the taco chair, a box of tissues in her hands, tears rolling down her face, while the television spooled through those endless clips of the first plane hitting the tower. There are moments where the brain struggles to catch up with the reality in front of it. I got as far as, "What's wrong?" before the second plane hit, and something in my stomach lurched.

"Sit down and watch," Heather mustered, and thrust a handful of tissues at me. We sat like that for hours, watching the chaos and the carnage, the planes hitting the towers over and over again, each time certain that they *had* to miss, that this *couldn't* be real. And then watching on-the-street interviews with ash-covered first responders, seeing the bodies pulled from the rubble, the families searching for their missing loved ones. We all remember what that day was like. We all remember the way the grief seemed to swell and burst and swell again, waves of fear and rage. How could this happen to us? To the United States of America?

After a while, there was just rage.

I couldn't understand how this had happened. I couldn't imagine who these people could be, these psychopaths out to scar the greatest country in the world. It felt like waking up to realize that the villains of your childhood were somehow real, and that true evil was capable of hijacking an airplane. I can't remember a time that I've ever been angrier.

Everyone knew that we couldn't let this attack go unanswered. War was coming. It was only a matter of time.

The weekend after 9/11, my unit met for a drill. I drove up to Laramie the night before, a chaotic bundle of nerves and fury and uncertainty. Was this the weekend that we'd be called up? I wanted to go—I wanted to strike swiftly and decisively, to unleash the same chaos and carnage on our enemies—but war is dangerous, and I'd be lying if I said I hadn't spent some of that week in a cold sweat over the possibility of dying in some foreign desert.

It seemed like everyone had had that same thought. No one was in the mood for dancing that night. We crashed in our cots and slept fitfully.

The next morning, after our first formation, I was wandering around the armory, trying to avoid the sergeant's make-work eye, when I happened upon Jake, hunched over the unit's computer, reading a news article on the 9/11 attacks. As the sergeant's tuneless whistle announced his approach, Jake switched the screen to the eerie green of the army's inventory tracking software, and I leaned in close. Hoping we looked busy.

A tense moment as the soft tap of our superior's footsteps came close . . . and then receded.

I breathed a little easier and glanced at Jake, who hadn't pulled away. He was inches from me and apparently uncon-cerned by it. What did it mean? What should I say? There was only one thing that sprang to mind, but the moment I said it, I kicked myself. "After this week, what do you think will happen to us?"

Jake's expression went strangely serious. "I think you should pack your things and call your family," he said. "This is it. We're heading out soon."

"What? Really?" A chill washed over me. I thought of Heather, waiting for me to come back, and my parents—whom

31

I hadn't even spoken to since the towers—losing their minds with worry. Signing up to drill one weekend a month was one thing, but potentially losing your daughter in war was something totally different. "Holy shit!"

I bolted. I ran right across the armory floor to the only face I knew was friendly—a girlfriend I'd connected with a couple of months back—and blurted out the news. I completely missed Jake's face sinking as he realized that I'd taken him seriously, and over the sound of my boots on the drill hall floor, I hadn't heard him call after me, trying to fix it.

My friend and I were freaking out, our fears running at top speed, when one of Jake's buddies caught up with me, a sheepish smile on his face. "Hey guys, before you freak out too hard," he said, totally failing to conceal his embarrassment, "Jake wanted me to tell you he was joking."

"Are you *kidding* me?" I didn't punch him. I want to make that clear. "I nearly pissed myself. What the hell kind of 'joke' is that?"

The guy just grinned awkwardly and backed away.

"Your friend is an *ass*, dude. Just so you know." So much for Jake being handsome and charming and decent.

But later that evening, after drill, Jake came up to me. I was more than ready to tell him to sit and spin, but he looked so nervous. Don't judge me, but it was kind of cute. "I'm really sorry about earlier," he started. "I don't know why I thought that would be funny... I guess with everything that's happened, I chose the wrong way to let off a little tension."

"No kidding," I said. "You make jokes about people's dead dogs too?"

32

"Totally fair, I get it, but honestly, I figured it wouldn't even work." His eyes were a vivid shade of blue. "Are you always that gullible, or was this just a blind spot for you?"

"And you were doing so well," I said, turning on my heel.

He reached out and took my wrist. "No, wait, look—I want to make it up to you. Can I make you dinner tonight?"

I turned back, looking him in the eye. One part of me was still deeply pissed. I've never been bothered by being the butt of a joke, but this was different. The other part of me had wanted this to happen for weeks. I'd imagined fifty different ways it could go. And his eyes were so inviting. Ugh. "Fine. It'd better be actual dinner, though. One more 'funny' trick and I will *make you pay.*"

"Understood," he said, with the first real smile I'd seen on him that weekend.

* * *

I don't usually get nervous before dates—before that evening, they'd never really gone anywhere, after all—but Jake had a bunch of roommates that I'd never met, and that's the kind of situation that makes me uncomfortable, just like the first time at the bars in Fort Collins. And, I'll admit, I really wanted this evening to go well. Unfortunate sense of humor aside, I was pretty sure that Jake was a good guy. I didn't want to be the person who screwed up a good thing.

Jake's place was a purple ranch house in the middle of Laramie, a block from the University of Wyoming campus. It had a huge porch and a welcoming living room that, when I walked in, was filled with his roommates and their friends, just hanging out, drinking. It sounds silly now, but the crowd was intimidating. September in Wyoming is when the weather starts to chill, so I was wearing a big winter coat over my short shorts, and as their eyes turned to me, I pulled that coat closer to me, an extra barrier between myself and their curious faces. I'm not great at striking up conversations with strangers, and I wasn't ready to open up to a room full of people I didn't know. Call it my sheltered upbringing. I made my way to the kitchen, my coat crunching and crinkling as I squeezed past the crowd.

Jake was making some sort of chicken and pasta dish, and I've got to admit, I was surprised. "Wow, you're actually cooking," I said, trying to find somewhere out of the way to stand. "I half expected to show up and find takeout containers in the trash."

"If I couldn't cook, I just would have taken you out for dinner," he said, and grinned. "This isn't my best dish—but it's good for a crowd. Maybe sometime you'll come back, and I'll make you something really special."

I smiled at him. "Hey, I'm already impressed. My cooking skills don't extend beyond fried egg sandwiches and boxed macaroni and cheese."

"Nothing like a good fried egg sandwich," he said, and did something complicated with spices.

"Yeah, well . . . a dude who knows his way around the kitchen. What else have you been hiding from me?"

He looked up at me with a dangerous smile that sent my heart racing. "Stick around, maybe you'll find out."

Dinner ended up being a group affair: his roommates and friends all filed into the kitchen, took a portion, and returned to the living room. Plate in hand, I lingered in the doorway, working up the courage to join them. I needn't have worried—with a nod, Jake drew me through and sat with me on an out-of-the-way couch. Around us, Jake's roommates were describing their latest adventures in Vedauwoo, a local hotspot for climbing. I couldn't focus on anything apart from how close my knee was to his.

As people finished their meals and went their separate ways, the living room grew quiet and began to feel a little more intimate. Jake and I could talk without involving the whole house, and we did our best to get to know one another.

The basics, about this man who sat tantalizingly close to me: (1) Jake had grown up in a Chicago suburb, which meant he was enchanted by my rural upbringing, as though I'd been raised in some sort of fairyland. (2) He'd joined up with the National Guard at around the same time as me. (3) He was studying engineering at the University of Wyoming in Laramie, and he was looking forward to graduating in the spring.

And then he asked me if I wanted to see his workshop.

I don't know how he knew. I like to think that he didn't, that he was just so proud of his work that he'd have shown anyone, but the fact is that the mere existence of a workshop that he identified as his was enough to sweep me off my feet. To explain: my dad had his own shop. He'd spent the whole of my childhood building and fixing and inventing useful little things that made his house homey and gentle and functioning. And because Jake had his own workshop—which he quickly let me tour—I suddenly knew that Jake had the same attention to detail, dedication, and creativity that my dad had modeled for me my whole life. "By their works shall you know them," after all. Jake's workshop gave me a view of his personality—of his soul, even—that I couldn't have gotten from hours of conversation.

Leaning against a sawhorse, my hand playing idly with Jake's latest creation, I locked eyes with him and said something I'd never said to another man: "You want to get out of here?"

We decided on a bar. I was feeling a little disadvantaged: I'd never been on the pursuing end before, and alcohol was the only way to even the field. Jake drove, a gigantic, cherry red Chevy 4x4. I had to keep his interest, so I started talking about all the things I enjoyed: biking, running, and fishing. At some point, I realized he was grinning to himself and I was instantly sure that he'd seen through my list, that he knew how much I wanted him—but no. He came right out and said that all the things I love doing are the same things he loves doing. He's just as addicted to sunshine and endorphins as I am. Years later, Jake would admit to me that as I was listing off my interests, he was hit with the premonition that he was sitting next to the woman who would be his future wife.

The rest of the night was a haze of drinks and darts and dancing. Drinks, to lubricate our senses and dull our anxieties about screwing up. Darts, because it let us talk and try to impress each other with our skills. And dancing, because at some point the subterfuge wore off, and all we wanted to do was get closer.

I know I've told you about how my dancing style is unique, based on fun instead of sexiness, and that's still true. But every dance should match its circumstances, and that night, Jake and I weren't dancing for fun. All of the sudden, I understood why those girls in the bars in Fort Collins were dancing the way they were. Call it grinding, call it bumping, we got close enough for me to feel the change in his jeans pockets. And that was when it happened.

I turned, just for a moment, moving and shaking and generally being as sexy as a woman can be, and saw Jake's head coming toward me, his mouth open, his eyes intent. He wanted me, and I knew I wanted him. My very first kiss was imminent.

And I dodged.

CHAPTER 3

A Series of Firsts

*C*amp Anaconda, Iraq. June 2003.

"Hey Koster," I call from the driver's seat, as our convoy creeps through the serpentine barricades of the camp entrance. "Want to see if you can get a block of ice from haji?"

Every camp has a series of alternating barricades that force vehicles to slow down and maneuver carefully, designed to stop vehicles from racing up to the camp at high speeds. We were headed out on our first real mission and already at 6:00 a.m., it was unbearably hot. I wanted some cold water, and haji (what we called pretty much anyone we saw in the Middle East) was the only source of ice around. The locals were everywhere. They'd long figured out how to take advantage of our deliberately delayed pace: it was an extended opportunity to sell us their crap. The closer we got to the exit, the more vendors we saw. They sold everything. From precious ice to cigarettes and booze, they had cornered the market on things soldiers wanted to make life a little easier.

"I'll see if I can grab some," Koster says, preparing for the moment, "but you gotta slow down more this time, those blocks are heavy."

I make some noncommittal noises. The pace of the convoy is the pace of the convoy, and there's only so much a driver can stall.

"What do you think? Two bucks?"

"Yeah, just get it, would you? I'm roasting already."

I slow the truck down a little, hoping it's slow enough for the hand-off, as Koster opens his door, waves a couple dollars at the ice guy and points at the ice in his wagon. The locals sell these huge blocks of ice, probably a foot square and two to three feet long. A couple days back, on the way into the base, we had tried this same maneuver and the ice had come crashing down during the hand-off, a tragic loss. This time, we're doing it right.

Koster haggles with his usual exaggerated style and gets the ice guy to bring us a quarter block, all while our semi sloooooowly creeps down the road. Koster snags the ice and gives the guy his money, wrestling the block into our newly acquired Styrofoam cooler. I look over at the ice. To say that it's murky doesn't quite cover it; there are chunks in there. But we don't need to drink it, we just need it to keep our stuff cold.

In the evening, after we've delivered our load of supplies to a remote FOB (forward operating base), Koster and I need to reload the cooler. With Koster driving, I'm in the hot seat now, my turn to negotiate the trade. But as we approach the camp entrance, we see soldiers frisking the vendors outside the gate, tossing carts of *goods, and inspecting blocks of ice. Koster maneuvers through the obstacle course and as we get close to the gate guards, I lean out the window. "Hey, what's going on with all the hajis?"*

"One of them was selling blocks of ice with frozen hand grenades in them," the guard shouts back to me. "You can still get some, but make sure you can see through it."

That could have been us.

That was the first time I really felt how close the danger was.

* * *

First kisses are meant to be romantic and fantastical—like snow falling in the moonlight, or a sunrise after surviving an adventure. Beauty, enchantment, and perfection. They're *not* supposed to happen after a couple of drinks and half an hour of grinding on the local bar's dance floor.

But I didn't freak out and push him away, or anything like that. I just set things up so that when he leaned in to kiss me, he missed. And he seemed okay with it. He didn't call me a prude or ditch me. He just went back to dancing, like nothing had happened.

The drive back to the armory was quiet. The wide truck cab, swallowing up all my anxious little hems and haws, trying to put us back where we were before The Attempt. He didn't even put on the radio. Finally, I couldn't take it anymore. "I'd never been, y'know, *kissed*, before," I said, wishing it sounded cooler. Wishing he understood how important this was.

"Wait, seriously?" he said, skeptically. "You've never kissed anyone?"

"It's not you."

"I've seen you out at the bars, you're always with someone."
I shrugged.

"Never?"

"Yeah, seriously. It's my first time."

"Okay, well," he still looked a little skeptical. "If you want our first kiss . . . I mean your first kiss, to be special, then I want that too."

"Oh," I said, stunned. "Oh."

The next weekend, Jake came down to Fort Collins, and I showed him the town. When the night was over, we came back to the apartment. I'd never had an overnight guest before, and I was a little tipsy, so it's possible that I left Jake on the couch and promptly "forgot" about him. I'd brushed my teeth, changed into my pajamas, and fallen into bed before realizing I was missing something. And that was when I heard the knock at my bedroom door. At my invitation, Jake stepped in. "Would it be okay if I slept in here tonight?" he asked. "With you?"

It was a strange moment. We hadn't even kissed yet, and here he was asking if he could spend the night in my bed. People always tell you that you can't trust boys, that they can't help themselves, that you've got to protect yourself. But this was Jake. And even though we'd only really connected a week before, I was sure that I *knew* him. That I could trust him. That all that other stuff was crap. I knew myself and I knew my sister was in the next room. I wasn't ready for anything more than sleeping, and I trusted that Jake understood.

So, I made some room for him on my tiny bed, and he wrapped his arms around me. Lying there like that, we fit together like a hand in a glove. We stayed there the entire night, his arms wrapped tight around my little body, fast asleep.

In the morning, we packed up a couple of backpacks for ourselves and for Jake's dog, Barley. Jake's most loyal sidekick, Barley was a stumpy-tailed cattle dog with orange-and-white fur and a lapdog delusion, despite his size. I was in love with him and told this to Jake at every opportunity.

Jake's 4x4 brought us up the mountain, its four-wheel drive keeping us moving through the deep snow. It was a terrifying journey, with a couple of close calls, but Jake knew how to cope with the mountain roads. He got us to the trailhead, safe and sound, and, I'll be honest, seeing my man operate his machine like that was sexy as hell.

Jake had planned a snowshoeing adventure for us. I'd never tried it before, and at first, it was a little awkward trying to lift those big, flat snowshoes, walking without accidentally kicking yourself, and so on. But the day was glorious. Cold and crisp, a gentle breeze of fresh mountain air, and the sun shining down on sparkling snow. We tromped along the trails, cracking jokes at each other and laughing, until we reached a lookout point with a view of the valley below, snow-bright and vast.

"It's beautiful," I said, and I took his hand.

And then we kissed.

It was perfect. The view of the valley before us. The packed snow beneath our snow shoes. Barley frolicking in a nearby drift, totally unaware that this was the sort of moment that changes lives. I couldn't have imagined it any better. Jake's lips tasted of honey, and his scent clung to me for days afterwards.

The months passed. The news was full of Operation Enduring Freedom, the campaign against the Taliban in Afghanistan. We waited, stressing every time the phone rang, but our orders never came. And in the meantime, Jake and I spent as much time together as we could.

About a month into our relationship, we were snowshoeing, and Jake fell behind. When I went back for him, I realized that he'd stomped out "I LOVE YOU" in the snow. The sudden switch in emotion—from worry and annoyance to breathless romance—filled my eyes with tears. I said, "Thank you," and Jake looked disappointed, and a little confused. He wanted me to say it back. Hell, *I* wanted to say it back. It was certainly true enough. But I wanted to wait my turn—to tell him when I couldn't hold it back anymore—not just because he'd said it to me. I didn't wait long. He was heading back to Laramie that night, and as I kissed him goodbye, I whispered those all-important words in his ear. There's a difference between knowing how someone wants you to feel and feeling it yourself. When it comes to love, you *have* to feel it yourself. You can't let anyone tell you how you feel.

For me, loving Jake was apparent by how much his absence hurt. It *hurt* when he was gone. A physical pain that lived in my chest. But when he was with me, it was as if fireworks were going off 24/7. Moment after moment of joy and wonder.

As far as I was concerned, I'd met the man I was going to spend the rest of my life with. We might as well have been married—except for one important thing.

A couple of months into dating—just a little while after bringing out the L-word—Jake told me he had something special planned for our next weekend together. "Make sure you pack some nice evening wear," were his exact words, and then he refused to tell me where we were going. I didn't have much in the way of "evening wear," so, after briefly flirting with idea of sewing some curtains together, I got my sister involved. If nothing else, she'd go shopping with me.

She did a lot more than that. "A fancy weekend away?" she began, "It's nice of him, but you know what he's going to expect in return, right?"

I knew what *other* guys would want in return, but Jake was different. Or at least, I thought he was. This was the same guy who'd been cool with me dodging his kiss, who'd spent a whole night in my bed just holding me. "Jake is the perfect gentleman," I said, the picture of indignation. "He would never."

Heather smirked knowingly. "Sure. Never."

I want to tell you that my faith in Jake's honor never flagged, but . . . a sister can get in your head. Jake and I made it halfway to the airport before he broke down and told me where we were going: Las Vegas. He's never been able to keep any secret from me for too long. And the tiny version of my sister that has always occupied the cynical part of my brain just rolled her eyes and pointedly didn't say, "I told you so."

I never expected to visit Las Vegas. I wasn't sure what I'd do there. I'm not enthusiastic about gambling or prostitutes. And considering everything I'd ever seen or read on the subject, I wasn't sure what else Vegas had to offer.

But I was excited. Jake was with me, he thought we would have a good time, and I was willing to trust him.

When the plane landed, I learned a couple new things: First, Las Vegas is way more serious about gambling than I expected.

I mean, I knew that it was a serious industry, but I didn't know that it was slot-machines-in-the-airport serious. Who'd even think to put slot machines in an airport terminal? How does the mind even get to that place? The second thing I learned was that the people who had gotten to the place were hooked. The airport slot machines were *busy*. I'd have thought that people in an airport would be concerned about getting on their flights—but no. Their attention was on the spinning dials and flashing lights.

I didn't understand it. I don't think I ever will. But knowing that people can be *this* different from me has to be worth something.

We had a room at the Excalibur—the medieval-themed hotel—but we started off the day by getting breakfast at the Luxor. Everyone always says that the Las Vegas buffets are insane, and I must admit, they weren't wrong. Seafood, steak, cinnamon rolls . . . we stuffed ourselves beyond recognition. To walk some of it off, we wandered down the Strip, taking in the shops, the casinos, the famous fountain, and the costumed populace—from elaborately dressed showgirls to Elvis impersonators—until my senses were completely overpowered.

We went to a show at Bally's, which was all rhinestones and topless showgirls—I thought I might have to pry Jake's jaw off the floor for him—and then we got dinner in the Eiffel Tower at the Paris resort

It was fancier than I expected it to be, and pricier. Remember, we were twenty-two years old. My budget might have extended to a drink in this place, but not much more. But this was Jake's party, and he was splurging. He just wanted me to sit back and enjoy it.

None of which helped my anxieties about his "expectations."

When is it "right" to have sex? I know that at church, we were taught that you should wait until you're married. That sex was only for married people. I always figured that that was what was expected of me, and I didn't disagree. However, I knew—just as much as Jake did—that we would eventually be married, so why should I let something like a marriage certificate decide when I want to do something? But that spawned a bigger question: How do I know when I *want* to have sex? And how do I rank my own wants within the moral framework that had shaped me from childhood? What will having sex do to our relationship, and the expectations I have for myself?

That night, we didn't do it. Not to say we didn't have some fun.

Jake might have been disappointed, but he didn't show it. He didn't even mention the idea.

How do you know when you're ready? I loved Jake. I trusted him. He was smoking hot, and I knew that I wanted him, but didn't there have to be something else? Some sign that I was ready?

But there was nothing. For months, there was just the gentle pressure from my own libido and the warmth of Jake's eyes. And I had so many questions that I couldn't bear to ask. If we did have sex, would he think differently of me? Would he think I was a slut, maybe? What if he didn't like having sex with me? What if I didn't like having sex with him? What if I didn't like having sex at all?

It took a conversation with my sister late one night to work it through. Heather had been dating Rick for ten years.

She'd even lived with him for some of that time, those strange awkward years in Des Moines. But now he was in Denver. Moving out to Fort Collins had meant that she had a little less distance now, but they still saw each other about as often as I saw Jake.

"But nothing ever happens!" she complained. "It's like we spend time together and talk, and it's just about day-to-day stuff: 'My day was fine, how was yours?'"

"So?" That sounded like every married relationship. I couldn't see what was wrong.

"So . . . we aren't married. We don't live together. We aren't building any kind of future together. We're just rolling along, like happiness happens automatically."

This sounded weird. With Jake and me, happiness more or less *was* automatic. It felt like we *were* moving toward a future together. What was she getting at? "Isn't that the way it goes?"

"No," she said. "The only pieces of life that *just happen* to you are the bad ones. If you want your life to go well, you've got to make it happen yourself."

I lay awake late that night. Heather was right. All of the pieces of my life that I'm happiest with, or proudest of, came from the times when I made a deliberate change to my life. Going to college. Joining the Guard. Falling in love with Jake. Each time, I'd had to step outside of the life that I had. I'd had to do something new.

The next weekend, I was up at Jake's place, lying in his bed, watching the way his muscles moved as he put on a shirt, when I realized I'd already made my decision.

"Jake," I said, "I'm ready."

He turned around so quickly that he nearly fell over. "Ready-ready? Or ready for bed ready?"

I grinned. "Ready-ready. Never been surer of anything in my life."

* * *

Jake wanted it to be perfect, so we decided to wait until the next day, after drill. Jake had a whole plan that he refused to tell me, so I got to spend the day contemplating the possibilities and wondering if the scanty sex ed I'd gotten in high school was accurate. I also felt the old surge of insecurities—what if I'm no good? What if Jake is no good? How will I know what counts as "good"? And so on. I tried to tamp it all down, but sexual fears are inescapable. I was on edge the whole day.

When the time finally came, Jake called me down to his bedroom. He had Norah Jones singing romantically from his stereo. He'd lit the whole room with candles. He'd drawn a warm bath and strewn it with rose petals.

It was straight out of every girl's romantic fantasies.

After the bath, I joined Jake on the rose petal–covered bed. Close together and warm from the bath, I was exactly where I wanted to be—but something was off. I looked around. Rose petals. Candles. My man, naked beside me. Romantic music. That was it. It was all so traditional, so expected. And this felt too storybook for me.

Before Jake could get too far, I stopped his hands. "Babe, you know I love Norah Jones," I said, "but for my first time, why don't we listen to something else?"

"Like what?"

49

I cast around, looking for something that fit. My eye fell on one of his CDs. "How about Nine Inch Nails?" Since college, heavy metal music had always made me feel rebellious and aggressive, and the more I thought about it, the more I realized it made me feel a little bit naughty. That was what I wanted.

Jake vaulted out of bed and made it happen, and then he came back to bed, and . . . we made each other happy.

CHAPTER 4

Commitment

Camp Tallil. May 2003.

The truck pulls to a halt. I look around, wondering why we're stopping here. "Hey, Koster, where do you think we will spend the night?"

"I don't see a single standing structure anywhere," he says, his eyes taking in the same desolate wasteland as mine. The base we'd just pulled into is bombed out, nothing but piles of rubble. We get out of the truck and hear Top calling everyone to form up on him.

"Welcome to your first night in Iraq," Top says, and launches into a monologue about our first night in a war zone and how we should observe all the rules of engagement and maintain situational awareness, and so on and so on. "We have a long, dangerous mission ahead of us," he says, wrapping up, "and it's my expectation that we will ALL be here together on our last night as well." And finally, the kiss-off: "We'll be spending the night" right here and leaving early in the morning. Get some sleep."

It's the first night that we are really on our own, away from the luxury of running water, a roof over our head, and chow halls. Dark comes on, quiet as ever, and we leave the formation, heading toward our trucks. I pull out my cot and sleeping bag, careful not to let them drop into the sand, fine as talcum powder. The sand got everywhere within minutes of stepping off the trucks, and I don't want to sleep with it in my bag.

"Where do you want to set up?" Jake asks, coming out of the dark with his own cot and bag.

"I don't know," I say. "We don't have many options. It's either in the sand, on the trailer, or in the cab."

"I'm done being in the cab of that truck today. And it's too hot, anyway."

"Trailer it is, then," I say. There's no way I'm staying down in the sand.

We pitch our cots on top of the flat-bed trailer and set up our bags. It's too hot to sleep in them, but there is something comforting about sleeping on top of one. We set up our stuff, grab an MRE, and head toward our platoon.

A few soldiers are crowded around with their MREs, talking about the sights of the day. There's a rumor flying around that someone saw a guy with an AK as we drove through a little border town. I am exhausted and a little disoriented, unsure of how to cope with my new surroundings. It's difficult, adjusting to a new place. Even more so when that new place is a flat-bed trailer in a bombed-out Iraqi air base. Jake and I excuse ourselves from the meal, and head for our cots.

I go to wash my face and realize how hard it is to pour water from a bottle with one hand and try to wash your face with the other. In the end, Jake pours the water as I wash up, and I do the same for him. We're going to have to work together on even the simplest everyday tasks in this new life.

* * *

"You sure you want me to take these?"

Heather stood over a box, ready to lay a strip of packing tape down and claim it as hers. The box contained the neon signs she and I had bought when we first moved in.

I puffed a sigh up through my bangs. "Yeah, take 'em. Jake's place already has stuff all over the walls, and neon bar signs aren't really his style."

"They're your style, though. More than mine."

"Take 'em. Really. I'd just end up bringing them back to the pawnshop."

The sun was just going down. We were surrounded by packing foam and bubble wrap. Jake was driving down tomorrow to bring my stuff up to his place in Laramie, while Heather was moving out to our friend Jeff's house across town. To help us pack, we had a couple of disposable cups and a bottle of Smirnoff Ice.

"This is the right move, right?" asked Heather, easing back against a roll of bubble wrap.

"Sure," I said, "Isn't it? Jake and I are rock solid, and this is the next step. And you and Rick . . . you're always saying that you need to move forward. Maybe you moving in with Jeff will get Rick to put his ass in gear."

"Maybe. I don't know. It's just . . . we've had a lot of fun here. I'm going to miss you. I'm going miss *us*."

I pulled her into a bear hug. "It's just Laramie. A couple hours away, at most. We'll see each other all the time." Both of us knew this was a lie, but what else could I say? The truth hurt too much.

The next day, amidst Jake showing up with his truck and Heather filling up her sedan, our goodbyes were quick. We'd said everything we needed to say, and now there were just the twin aches of change and homesickness. We couldn't dwell too long on it, or we'd both fall apart.

So, together, Jake and I made the long drive up to Laramie. We carted all my stuff into his room in the purple house, and I set about unpacking. For a long time, I had thought that sex was the peak of intimacy for a couple, but moving in with Jake quickly proved me wrong. There's no way you can know everything about a man if you only ever see him on weekends. Within the first two days of living with Jake, we'd learned more about each other than we had the whole time we were dating. I was irritated that he had little regard for spending and almost no food on hand, and he was annoyed with my lax attitude toward dishwashing, so much so that I felt like he was ready to start breaking every dish in the house, just so we'd be forced to buy new ones.

I didn't have a lot of stuff—clothes mostly, my roller blades, and a mountain bike—but even so, moving into someone else's space was kind of weird. I had to shove aside a bunch of Jake's clothes in the closet and find room in the shower for my self-care stuff. Wherever you go, your stuff expands to fit your space, so my moving in made things a little more cramped for both of us.

As we settled in together, we figured out that we were both pretty laid back. Jake made me feel at home by making us a solid oak bed frame in his workshop. We found a routine. Jake would go work at the National Guard Armory during the day, and in the evening we would venture out with Barley into the foothills surrounding Laramie.

I should have known that it couldn't last.

I was supposed to be job hunting when Jake got home from work that afternoon, but I was on the phone with my sister. That morning, my dad had had a ministroke. He was fine —no permanent damage—but it scared me nonetheless. I couldn't be there with him—we didn't have money for airfare, and my stepmother thought he'd throw a fit if he thought we were upending our lives to go sit in a hospital waiting room—but I couldn't focus. I wished that Heather were there with me. I wished that time could speed up—that I could blink and have my dad healthy and whole. It was the middle of May, perfect weather to be in the mountains. I wished more than anything that I could be out there; sunshine on my face, having an adventure with my man, confident again that everything would turn out fine.

When Jake opened the bedroom door, I was holding my phone in the dark and trying not to cry.

Jake could see—either from the way I wasn't really breathing or the way my face had gone red and splotchy—that something was wrong.

"What happened?" Jake asked, coming to sit beside me on the bed.

"It's my dad—he's in the hospital—a ministroke—" And the tears just about broke through.

"Do we need to go?"

"No, no, it's a ministroke." I tried to explain, but that was before WebMD or Wikipedia. All I knew was what I'd heard from my stepmother, everything third hand. All I really knew was that I couldn't go to him, and I couldn't stop worrying. Jake and I talked for a while, and then something in his face changed.

"Hey, you know how you've always wanted your own dog?"

"Um, yeah?" My sniffles paused to let me temporarily replace fear and worry with confusion.

"Let's go pick one out," Jake said, rising from the bed and looking for his keys.

"Wait, really?"

"Yeah." He turned to me, his face more determined than I'd ever seen it. "It might take your mind off things, and we wanted to do it soon anyway."

We're both very decisive people. When we want to do something, we do it. We don't hesitate, and we don't look back. But on the way to the local animal shelter, I could tell that something was on Jake's mind. He looked nervous.

"We don't have to get another puppy today, you know," I said, watching his face as he drove.

"Why would you say that?" He was grinning thinly. Something was definitely up. "I want one too."

"Okay. You just look like you've got something on your mind."

"Listen," Jake said, tight-breathed, his face flushing. "I was thinking. This isn't the right place for us—with my roommates and everything. Why don't we go somewhere else? Somewhere new?"

"But I just moved in a few weeks ago," I said, confused. I pulled back to meet his eyes. "I don't want to move to a whole new place and then move again after you graduate. That's just—"

"Yeah, but if that doesn't happen—"

"Wait, what?" There it was, that nervousness. Something he wasn't telling me. "If what doesn't happen?" I asked, trying to keep my voice from shaking.

He took a breath. Gripped the steering wheel tighter. "It looks like the University of Wyoming isn't going to let me graduate. They're kicking me out."

"Did you know this was happening?" I asked, my voice low and gentle.

"Sort of," he said. "I haven't been paying much attention to school lately."

I grimaced. Every day that he'd been down in Fort Collins with me, he hadn't been studying. "Is this my fault?"

I felt him sit up straighter, and he twisted away from me to look me in the eye. "No," he said, "I'm not going to let you think like that. My grades have been crap for a while now, and they've been that way because I haven't bothered showing up for more than half of my classes. This is on me."

I don't like saying that I felt relieved, but I did. I didn't want to be responsible for Jake's grades, but more than that, here was proof that Jake knew when the buck stopped with him. He wasn't trying to weasel out of responsibility or blame his misfortunes on anyone else. He'd tried to pretend they weren't real, for a while (and that was its own problem), but that's kind of what your early twenties are for. You make mistakes, and then you learn from them.

We pulled into the parking lot of the animal shelter, and Jake turned, looking at me with a touch of fear.

"Are—are you going to leave?" Jake's voice was close to cracking. I turned to look at him.

"What? Of course not. Why would you think that?"

He looked away.

"I'm not going to run away just because you got a few bad grades." I scooted over on the big bench seat of his truck, trying to wrap as much of my little body around him as possible, in the awkward space. "Just promise me. Next time something like this happens, let me know. We're a team. Don't hide this stuff from me."

His arm curled around me. "I promise," he said.

That day, we picked out a cute little cattle dog border collie mix, and I named him Cody.

* * *

Jake's little brother was scheduled to graduate from high school. I hadn't met any of Jake's family yet, but according to Jake, Jared was a cute kid, much taken with robots and Legos. I suspected that there was a bit of a gap between the Jared that Jake told me about and the young man getting ready to go to college.

We drove to Chicago the day before Jared graduated, and we stayed with Jake's parents. Meeting them for the first time was nerve-wracking. I don't usually pay a lot of attention to what people think of me, but I was hoping these were going to be my in-laws. I knew how to deal with new parental figures (you don't come out on the other side of both your parents divorcing and remarrying without some serious coping skills), but in this case, I knew that I couldn't take anything for granted. They weren't obligated to like me for the sake of their relationship with my mom or dad. They had no responsibility to see me grow up well. And if they wanted to, they could put a serious kink in my relationship with Jake. I really wanted them to like me.

Sure, they were nice enough, on the way to Jared's graduation ceremony and at the party that night, but at some point, between dessert and drinking a beer on the front porch, Jake told his dad that UW was kicking him out, and that was when things changed. Word spread quickly. Sitting quietly in the living room, I was playing a game of solitaire on the coffee table when the whole family trundled past the living room doorway, headed out to the porch. I wasn't sure if it was appropriate for me to follow—you know how it is to be a guest in a stranger's home—so I crept carefully after them, trying not to be seen.

Outside, in the quiet of an Illinois spring evening, Jake's parents were giving a gut-withering version of the disappointed-parent speech. It wasn't loud—they were clearly concerned that Jake had been kicked out of school—but I didn't have to hear it to see its effect on Jake: his shoulders slumped, his eyes firmly on his shoes. He'd let everyone down, especially his little brother Jared, who'd always admired and looked up to him. Every word hammered the point home. And then, through the mumble of disappointment and anger, I heard my name, and Jake's head snapped up. He said something—I don't know what it was—and then he turned and came inside. I scrambled to look as if I hadn't heard what was happening, but I don't think Jake noticed.

"You should pack up," he said. "We're leaving tonight."

And that was that.

It turned out that his parents were pushing him to come back home to Chicago and leave me behind. Did they think I was the reason he'd flunked a bunch of classes? Did they think I was the reason he got kicked out of UW? Did they think I was trying to keep him from fulfilling his potential, trying to dull his aspirations and drag him down into whatever Iowan hovel I'd crawled out of? I don't really know. But whatever they thought wasn't nice.

I was glad when we left. After seeing the effect of that conversation on Jake, I didn't feel comfortable staying there.

But that night, during the drive back to Laramie, there were still a lot of things to discuss.

"What do we do now?"

"I dunno," said Jake, his eyes on the road. "We don't owe anybody anything."

"Except the Guard," I said.

"Right."

"We can't stay where we are," I pointed out, "unless you want to just, I dunno, work in Laramie forever."

"Right." Jake was quiet for a minute. I watched the mountains pass through the window. "How about Albuquerque?"

"Excuse me?" Jake's suggestion seemed so far out of left field that I had trouble remembering that New Mexico was a *place*, let alone somewhere we could live.

"I've been wanting to go there for a while. And there's a decent university. And I heard that the New Mexico National Guard will pay for your classes if you go to college in the same state."

I gave him a long, appraising look. He'd clearly been thinking about this for a while. "Albuquerque," I said.

"Yeah."

It was one thing to move in with your boyfriend when he's got his own place and a stable job, but it was something else to move with him to someplace completely new and just start over. I sat for a moment with myself, looking for certainty. Did I love Jake enough to just pack up and leave with him? Did I love him enough to say goodbye to everything I'd ever known?

Who was I kidding? Of course I did.

"Let's do it," I said.

CHAPTER 5

On Our Own

I was panicking. It was rush hour on Interstate 40, and cars were weaving in and out of traffic, a situation that would have been frustrating if I hadn't been so terrified. Albuquerque was the biggest city I had ever driven in, and I was ready to bail. We hadn't even seen our new place. "I can't drive in this traffic!" I yelled into my cell phone, not really caring if I deafened Jake on the other end. "I can't live here! I can't even get around!"

"Stop it! Just STOP IT!" Jake's voice was tinny over the phone's speakers, but harsher than I was used to. "There's nothing you can do now but hang up your phone and follow me." I let my phone drop into my lap and focused on keeping up with Jake's truck, which was darting in and out of traffic, oblivious to the horrors that surrounded us. I'd forgotten I was following a Chicagoan.

* * *

We'd taken an apartment with a view of the mountains, which wasn't too shabby considering we'd rented it over the phone, without actually seeing it. My history with FedEx had gotten us a couple jobs working the early shift for the local warehouse. This meant that we headed into work just as our neighbors were getting home from an evening of dancing and bar-hopping, and we were not adjusting well. After a month or so of dealing with the early-morning cockroaches and our equally disgusting coworkers, Jake and I just . . . quit. There had to be better ways to support ourselves, we were sure.

Admittedly, we made this decision in the heat of the moment—that five-second period between hearing your alarm go off at 1:15 a.m. and throwing the clock against the wall. We hadn't wanted to get up that morning, we decided, and that meant that our income stream dried up like someone had turned off the tap. And rent and bills had no respect for our sleep cycles, sadly.

This may have never happened to you, but a funny thing occurs when you're young and healthy and suddenly free of society's expectations: You stop caring so much about what the correct thing to do is. I'd had a taste of that before; my earlier decision to put a pause on pursuing the rest of my BA was one of the most satisfying decisions I've ever made. I knew that trying to force myself into the wrong mold would only leave me miserable. Better to struggle for a while and eventually find the career that fit me.

Well, this was struggling. No jobs, no income; it was stressful. We had to sell or pawn some of our "valuables" to make rent.

But I was with Jake, so I knew everything would end up okay. Being jobless meant that we could spend the whole day together, cycling or hiking in the foothills, playing with the dogs in the park, and generally finding adventures in and around Albuquerque. If we didn't think about our dwindling bank accounts, it was an idyllic time. We spent beautiful days together, and at night we kept each other warm against the chill of the desert.

But it couldn't last forever. Technically speaking, it couldn't last more than a couple of days. There's only so long you can survive on the remains of your last-minute garage sale or the impromptu gambling lark that nets your boyfriend an extra hundred dollars. Sooner or later, the money runs out.

We weren't going back to FedEx. Even if they wanted us back—which, let's be honest, after quitting as suddenly as we did, they didn't—I wasn't ready to make those life sacrifices again. So, one quiet Sunday, as we stared at a utility bill we couldn't pay, we decided that the time had come. We both hit the want ads, and I started to really focus on what I could do to keep us afloat.

While Jake combed through construction sites and appliance salesman positions, I started thinking about waitressing. I had zero experience, but I knew that this wasn't going to be a permanent career path. Some servers turn the whole experience into this dance of grace and information—I was never going to be one of them. But we needed money. My requirements were: easy waitressing, plus copious tips.

I wish I could tell you that a job fitting these requirements, which also made my mother proud, was easy to find. But that would be a lie.

I also wish I could tell you that in my innocence, I'd never once considered strip club work, that the idea of taking a job in one of these clubs was so foreign to me that at first blush, I'd thought it was a strange little joke my brain had farted out, like a dream. But the truth is that we'd driven past a strip club the night before, and I had wondered aloud at how a place so blatantly in violation of every social norm we knew could not only continue to exist, but franchise itself. Jake smirked at my naiveté—he was pretty well-acquainted with the economic force that strip clubs thrived on. I just wanted to make some good tips.

I called to ask if they were hiring, and got an interview for that very day.

When I arrived, the club felt like a cross between Coyote Ugly and Moulin Rouge that had been scaled down, leaving all of the tragedy, none of the romance. At 2:00 p.m., the place was quiet and dark. I knew that most of a strip club's business happened during the night, but still, I was surprised. I'd expected one or two patrons slumped on the bar, left over from the night before, or at least a janitor, pushing a mop through cigarette butts and napkins, all while muttering obscure wisdom into his overalls. But no. Finally, I made a bit of noise—of all places, there was a service bell on the bar counter.

From somewhere upstairs, a voice shouted down to me. "Go ahead and take a seat!"

I found a clean-ish chair, somehow profoundly glad I'd decided to leave my black light at home, and sat myself down. A rough-looking, bleached-blonde forty-something finally emerged and took a seat in the chair across from mine. "Is this how you typically look?" was her opening volley.

I glanced down at myself. I'd worn jeans and a nice top—respectable clothes, but nothing you'd mistake for formal wear. "Yes?" I said.

She snorted and subjected me to what I can only describe as some of the most intense scrutiny I've ever endured. "You're going to have to step up your game," she said. "You'll need some tall boots with high heels, heavier makeup—subtle, naturalistic looks don't hold up under the lights—and our company shirt. It comes in a cropped tee or tube top."

It took me a second to realize that I'd been hired as a waitress at a strip club without so much as a work history, but I got past it, and chose the T-shirt.

When I got home and told Jake about my "interview," he couldn't believe that I intended to go through with this. But money is money, and I was going to do my part.

My first night was a couple of days later. My shift started at seven, so by the time Jake was home from wallpapering the town with his resume, I was all decked out in high-heeled boots, black miniskirt, and the required company tee. I'd pushed the envelope with my makeup, too, or at least I thought so. Jake could barely keep his hands off me. I should've taken this as a sign that I'd gone too far.

The long drive over gave me plenty of time to freak myself out. *I can't believe Jake was okay with me doing this. I can't I believe I'm okay with me doing this. Should I just turn around now? It's not too late.* My little sedan slid past street light after street light, obviously slower than the other cars on the road. Reluctant. *What would my family say? They'd say, "This isn't the little girl we raised. Little Heidi wouldn't subject herself to working at a sinful stripper club. We raised you better than this!"* They were right. Now that it came time to actually go through with it, what had seemed like a good idea now felt ominous and desperate. What should I expect? Will the girls have crabs? What other disgusting side effects of being around strippers should I be on the lookout for? And what do I do about the clientele? I was not looking forward to dealing with them. I'm not great at customer service under the best of circumstances, and these would probably qualify as the worst of circumstances.

I guess my new boss wanted to start me off easy. It was a weeknight, so business was pretty slow. The club itself was very dark when I arrived. I tried not to look around but headed straight upstairs. The locker room was packed with girls chit-chatting as they got themselves ready, some of them dressed, some of them not. I know that the locker room of my gym was bound to be occupied by women in various stages of undress, but it being the locker room of a strip club made it that much more *scandalous*. All of my usual getting-along-with-people skills evaporated, and I prayed that no one would talk to me. I headed downstairs to start my shift.

When I got to the floor, I realized that the previously dark club was finally jumping. The music was growing in volume, and at every turn, naked women were working their poles. I couldn't help but stare. This world was bizarre.

It wasn't like I was up on stage myself, but still, the suspicion that I was committing an awful sin just by being in the room was loud in my heart. This was not the job for me. That fact was suddenly very clear. I was way too uncomfortable. Every blood vessel in my body was urging me to head for the door. But I knew that as of that moment, Jake and I had no money. I needed to stick around and earn at least one paycheck.

I moved slowly through the club, looking for a safe spot to just be and collect myself, but every time I thought I'd found a hidey-hole, another waitress would come up from behind me and say something terrifying about how the real money came from getting up on stage or giving lap dances. It seemed like everyone had assumed that I'd been hired as a dancer and was just waitressing to get a feel for the club. They were all looking forward to seeing what I could do.

I was pretty confident that they were going to be disappointed.

I took up an out-of-the-way position near the bar, and tried to make myself look busy. A guy in his mid-forties was sitting nearby, drinking a beer, not even watching the show. He smiled and waved at me. At first, I figured he just wanted a drink—I was wearing the company shirt, after all—but when I got there, he just said, "First-day jitters?"

I couldn't believe I was that obvious. I nodded, and he gestured to the seat next to him for me to sit. I scanned the room: No one else looked like they needed an overwhelmed waitress, and my boss was nowhere in sight. I sat down.

I spent the next four hours talking to this guy about everything under the sun. We got going on life and religion and politics—all the important things people tell you to never talk about with strangers—and while we didn't agree on everything, I felt like it was a pleasant way to run out the clock. The whole time, he only ever looked at me. His eyes never strayed to the girls on stage. This is embarrassing, because looking back on it, I should have known something was up, but I didn't. Instead of being creeped out that a dude in a strip club was focusing entirely on me, I just felt flattered. Every so often, I'd go get a customer a drink, but I always came back to my seat next to this weird guy who, in a sea of naked women, only had eyes on me.

After a while, the guy paid his tab, left me a pretty nice tip, and headed out. I rode out the end of my shift, grabbed my stuff out of the locker, and headed for the door. And discovered the guy I'd been talking to hadn't gone home. He was just hanging out in the parking lot, waiting for my shift to be over. Needless to say, I stopped thinking of him as a kind and attentive ear for all my troubles and opinions, and I started thinking of him as a psychotic stalker.

I got Tom, the bouncer, to deal with it. I waited in the foyer, not sure what was happening, until Tom came back and gave me the all-clear. "That guy won't be an issue for you anymore," he said, and walked me to my car. I locked my doors from the inside and wondered what "won't be an issue anymore" meant, coming from Tom. He was a big, scary-looking guy. Was my stalker dead in a dumpster? Maybe he'd just scared him off?

Either way, I sped home that night, one eye perpetually on the rearview mirror, and I never went back to that club.

CHAPTER 6

What Do You Really Want?

One day after I got home from my new job as a customer service rep, I opened the mailbox to find an unusually fancy envelope. Heavy matte paper. Crisp square corners. It looked solid. Adult.

I dropped the rest of the mail on the kitchen table and sat. I'd known this was coming. Tiffany's wedding invitation. Strictly speaking, I'd signed up to be one of her bridesmaids, but that had been ten months ago. It might as well have been a lifetime.

Tiffany was my wildest friend. The one who made me late for class, who'd started drinking and going to senior parties years before I'd even considered taking a drink, who had "accidently" locked me out of my dorm room, while "studying" with a friend. She was also the one who'd kept all my secrets, remembered every one of my birthdays, and instantly believed in me when I announced I was joining the National Guard. She was my best friend, and I had been over the moon about being part of her wedding.

But a lot had changed since she got engaged. It wasn't anything between us—we talked on the phone every couple weeks, and kept up with each other—but something was different in me. I'd left Iowa as a kid, tagging along behind my big sister as we chased our dreams across the country, but now, after a stint working at a strip club, I was running customer service for a furniture store and living in sin with my boyfriend of eight months. I didn't have to say it aloud, but I could hear the way it would sound. Some old biddy in the back of the church would murmur it to her friends, a sneer practically dripping off every syllable, and everyone back home would think I'd failed. That I'd gone looking for adventure but found a tawdry, humdrum, little life.

I couldn't look at Tiffany's invitation for very long, so I set it in the napkin holder on the table and went for a run in the foothills until Jake got home from his new job as a computer salesman.

He'd barely set his bag down before he'd picked up the envelope. "Babe? What's this?"

I came back out to the kitchen, the sweat from my run dripping off my brow. "Tiffany's wedding's in a couple months." I didn't know how to hold my face—could he tell what I was feeling?

"Hmm." He pulled the invitation out, flipped it over to see the date. "Babe, I'm sorry—we're just getting back on our feet. I don't think we can afford to have both of us go." New jobs. No vacation time. And what about the dogs? He didn't need to say it. I shared his same concerns. It didn't change the fact that I still wanted him to be there with me.

"Right, I guess," I was backing up, my face already red, tears prickling behind my eyes. As he looked up, alerted by the tremble in my voice, I fled to the bedroom. On top of everything, I wouldn't even have him with me. I buried my head under a pillow.

"Heidi, babe, I need you to talk to me." When I looked, he was standing in the bedroom doorway, silhouetted by the hall light, his shoulders sloped, his head bowed.

I sat up, drew my knees to my chin. "Is this enough?" I asked, gesturing to the room, the apartment, everything. "Is it enough for you?"

He came closer, sat on the bed. Still obviously bewildered. "I mean, yeah? For now? We've got a place, and like, food, and we've got each other." He took my hand. "Is it not enough for you?"

And then I felt ashamed. Of course it was. I'd been happy—really, honestly happy—just five hours earlier. I ran a hand over my face to wipe away my tears. "I think it's just—for the wedding, I'll have to go home and tell people about us and . . . the reality of it is only just sinking in."

"Oh," he said, thoughtful. "Are you ashamed of me?"

"What? Of course not!"

"Are you sure, 'cause if your Iowan people are just like you, you know I won't fit in. I still don't know the difference between field corn and sweet corn, for instance."

I hit him with a pillow. "Anyone can tell the difference, you doof."

He smiled. He'd gotten me to smile. "Okay," he said, "then how can we make this better?"

I took a breath and thought. I was clutching a pillow to my chest, and my eyes fell on my hands. My painfully naked fingers. The thought struck me like a bullet. If I went home with *proof* that Jake and I were for real . . . I glanced up at Jake. Was this too bold?

Might as well find out.

"We could get me a ring, maybe?" I said, hoping it didn't sound too much like a question. Hoping the vague eventually-when-we-get-married conversations we'd had were as important to him as they were to me. Hoping he was right there with me on this might-as-well-admit-we're-soulmates island.

His face went serious, and my heart dropped out of my feet. He was going to say no. He was going to say that he was just with me for the good times. He was going to say that he hated me and wished I'd been dead for the last six months.

But instead, he said, "Did you want to start with that boutiquey-looking place on Main, or the Zales in the mall?"

"What?" I couldn't have heard him properly.

"Ring shops," he said. "I figure we can put it on the credit card and pay it down with the next couple paychecks."

It was a good thing he was already on the bed, because I tackled him.

* * *

That Friday, we took a field trip to the boutiquey-looking place on Main. I don't really wear jewelry, so the array of bright sparkly expensive things was incredibly overwhelming. After a moment of getting used to the shop itself, I started just

74

trying a bunch of rings on. I'd never spent much time thinking about what my engagement ring should be like—I know some girls do, but it was never really my thing—so I guess I was just waiting until one leaped out at me. Ring after ring, all different sizes, until finally my eye fell on The Ring. A gold band with a marquise-cut, half-carat diamond in the middle, with a sapphire on each side, each sapphire surrounded by smaller diamonds. It was the one.

Sometimes you just know.

Jake had the cashier ring it up, and he put the little velvet box in his pocket. I tamped down the impulse to slip it on my finger then and there; I knew that the proposal—the real proposal—was something Jake would want to plan himself.

It was a quiet Saturday evening in early fall, just as the nights were beginning to cool. Jake and I had spent the day on our bikes, thrashing through underbrush and wheeling through recently hydrated stream beds, rushing down the trail in the foothills. I had expected to get home, slip into my pajamas, and retire to the balcony with a drink and the dogs, letting the warmth of the sunset cool on my skin. But that wasn't in the cards.

We were hanging the bikes up when Jake, with studied nonchalance, said the following high-alert words: "You've got a really nice dress, right?"

There was no other interpretation, but what was I supposed to do? Dissolve into excited giggling and ruin the mood of his plan? *I know what you're doing! I know what's happening!* Of course not. So, keeping my breath even and my face serene, I said, "Yeah, I think so. I've got that sleeveless thing."

"Good," he said. "I was thinking we could go out tonight."

Of course you are. Of course we're going out. You're not going to propose in the apartment. But what I said was, "Okay. Where were you thinking?"

"It's a surprise," he said, and I thought, *Well, that's settled then. No doubt about it. We're getting engaged tonight.*

So I took a shower. I styled my hair as prettily as I could, curling it just so. I did my makeup as well as I knew how—contouring wasn't a thing back then, but I could pair dark eyeliner with a deep red lip as well as anybody—and I slid into my ivory shift-dress. Form-fitting and sleeveless, it went to just above my knee and made me feel elegant and capable. I paired it with a pair of little black heels and a faux leather jacket, and as I stood before the full-length mirror in our bedroom, examining the flattering way the dress clung to me, I felt like I had never been so ready for romance. Everything was falling into place.

I came out of the bedroom, trying to keep myself calm. This strange voice in my head was urging me to pretend this was all normal—that since Jake was pretending, I should too. But when Jake saw me, dressed as I was to the nines, his eyes went wide. I hadn't thought about how nervous he was—he'd done such a good job of playing casual—but in that moment, his guard dropped, and I knew we were in this together.

When we got outside, Jake opened the car door for me—a courtly gesture that underscored the significance of the trip—but tripped up a bit when he said, "Can I tell you where we're going?"

I looked at him. His cool had almost completely evaporated. When he's nervous, he tells me what he's nervous about—we've sort of always been like that—but this was one time when I knew he needed to keep his plan to himself.

This is the deal with proposals. Unless it's a complete surprise—the guy wakes up one morning just certain that he needs to propose, regardless of how his lady feels—a successful proposal is a team effort. Sure, the guy needs to have a plan—it should be something spectacular, something deeply romantic— but the girl needs to be prepared to let him make that plan happen. She needs to do whatever necessary to support that plan going well. And it can be hard, letting go enough to let him take the lead. There's a temptation to try to manage everything yourself, to feel like you can't leave something as important and romantic as the Moment You Got Engaged to someone else, even if that someone else is the man you already trust with your life. But that's kind of the deal. This is a big moment, and you've got to trust that your man can make it magnificent.

I had to support Jake's first impulse to make the events of that night a surprise. I knew that his plan involved me not knowing what was coming up, and if we were going to work together to make his vision of that night happen—a vision that I trusted would be beautiful and touching—I needed to help him stick to that plan. So when he asked me if he could tell me what was happening, I said, "Of course not. You have to keep this secret!"

He looked at me with puppy-dog eyes, but I wasn't budging. I wasn't going to give him an opening. He was perfectly capable of keeping his plan to himself, he just needed a little reinforce-ment. As I got into the car, I watched him take a big, reassuring breath, and then he closed the door after me.

This doesn't mean I wasn't curious, though. As Jake drove, we kept passing places that I thought would have made good proposal spots. Nice restaurants. Scenic lookouts. The turns to places that had been significant for us. But Jake kept driving. We were going east, toward the foothills, and we finally pulled into the Sandia Peak Tramway.

I'd wanted to try the tramway since we first arrived in Albuquerque, but I'd always been a bit of a fraidy-cat about it. A huge gondola, made to fit about ten people, the tramway follows a near-vertical path up the side of the mountain. For nearly two and a half miles, the gondola is suspended in midair. From beneath, you can sometimes see it rock back and forth, shuddering a little on the steel cables.

As we pulled into the parking lot, I turned to Jake, my face covered in a delighted grin. "Are we—" I began, breathlessly, pointing excitedly at the tramway. "Is that—?"

He smiled back at me—back in control of the plan—and said, "I thought you might like this."

If I hadn't been all dressed up, I'm pretty sure I would have been bouncing off the car walls.

Once we got to the gondola, though, it was a different story. The path up the mountain was so steep, and the cables going up looked so tiny in comparison. Like threads tying down a giant. My excitement flipped with my stomach, and I hesitated on the landing platform.

"Are we going?" Jake asked, when it became clear that my shoes had turned to cement.

"Right," I said, and kept standing there.

Jake scoffed a little—which somehow made me feel better, like we were just a couple kids standing on the edge of a diving platform—and he stepped onto the gondola. I saw it shift slightly beneath him, like he'd stepped into a canoe, and I let out one long, calming breath. He offered me his hand, and I suddenly knew that I couldn't leave him hanging like that. I took his hand and stepped into the gondola with him. At least, if we died, we'd die together.

Another half-dozen people crowded into the gondola around us, the motors began to whir, and the gondola took off. We stood together at the glass, watching as the ground fell away and the desert stretched out before us, the sunset painting the terrain in shades of orange and pink, the sky fading to purple. As we glided up the cliffside, our view of the valley grew, until we could see all of Albuquerque and miles beyond. The vastness of creation lay at our feet, and I threaded my fingers through Jake's, knowing that he was just as humbled by God's beauty as I was.

At the top of the tramway—more than ten thousand feet up—there is a nice restaurant and nothing else. Jake let me step off the gondola first, and together, we walked into the restaurant. From the outside, the building had looked warm and inviting, and now that we were inside, it was even lovelier. The walls and ceiling were decorated with elaborate woodwork. The lighting was dim, and there were candles at every table. Jake had made reservations, and the hostess led us to our table with a smile. I was enchanted by the restaurant, but I couldn't help wondering if this was his plan. Was he going to propose right here? In this—admittedly beautiful—dining room? In front of all these people? I wasn't ready for something this public. You see it in movies all the time—a waiter comes by with champagne, and there's a ring in the bottom of the glass, and then the man asks, and the whole restaurant erupts in applause—but I didn't want a crowd of people gawking at us during this important moment. I would be so embarrassed.

But our orders came, and nothing. We spent the meal amusing each other—reminding both of us that when this proposal happened, even if I was wrong about it happening that night, the reasons behind it were ironclad. We fit together. We belonged together. If either of us was stranded on a desert island and could only bring one other person, we would always choose each other.

When at last the check came, Jake wouldn't let me see it, but I knew it had to be more than we could afford. There was a tiny, anxious part of the back of my mind that fretted about the money—we were only just back on our feet, after all—but I couldn't really think about it. I was utterly preoccupied with wondering when he was going to propose. I was also trying to pretend to myself (somewhat unsuccessfully, I'll admit) that if tonight *wasn't* the night, I would be totally fine. That we'd just had a really nice dinner, and if Jake wanted to treat me like a princess *just because*, I was going to be glad about it. And maybe I would have been.

We stood up from the table together. I made vague gestures about heading for the door, but Jake stopped me. He took my hand, and drew me out to an area that overlooked the valley. The stars were out in force, competing with the lights of the city sparkling below.

It reminded me of our first kiss. I was turning to tell him so when I realized he was down on one knee.

"Heidi," he said, his eyes locked on mine, "I love you more than you will ever know. Will you marry me and make me the happiest man on earth?"

I know that I was expecting it, and that we'd already agreed and chosen a ring, but still. Tears ran down my face as I nodded and blubbered and cried, "Yes! There's nothing in the world I want more than to be your wife!"

He fit the ring on my finger, and just as I was holding it up to the restaurant's lamplights to inspect its glitter, he swept me up into his arms and kissed me.

It was a moment I'll treasure forever, retelling it over and over again. And once I'd described it to the people at home, the old biddies in Eagle Grove even started telling it to each other.

Over the next few days, we talked about all sorts of ways to get married, and all the places we dreamed about going on our honeymoon. We both knew that most of these ideas were out of reach, but we've always enjoy dreaming big. If only we'd known just how exotic and remote our honeymoon would actually be.

CHAPTER 7

The Fourth of November

When fall had rolled around, we'd both enrolled at the University of New Mexico. While it was a beautiful campus and I really did feel like I was trying, I just couldn't put my heart into it. I hate doing things halfway—my dad always says, "Either do it right, or don't do it at all." And I wasn't doing it right. I didn't feel like I fit in with the other students. Maybe it was that the school was too big, or maybe I just hadn't settled on a major. Either way, every day was uncomfortable. Just not the right fit. And Jake was beginning to feel the same way, particularly whenever he got off the phone with his parents.

One such night, I was struggling to stay awake while reading an exceptionally boring psychology textbook when he hung up the phone, and something about the slump of his shoulders let me know that he was upset.

"It's like nothing is good enough anymore," he said, plucking at the sofa arm. "Even when I'm 1,300 miles away, living on my own, they think I'm a kid they can straighten out with a stern talking-to."

I set the textbook aside. "What's the problem this time?"

He sighed. "Just the old bullshit about finishing school. They want me to go back to my engineering degree, but I'm like, 'Come on, there's a reason they kicked me out of engineering school at UW.' Honestly, I don't think I even want to do it anymore."

I went to join him on the couch, curling up under his arm. "So what do you want to do?"

"I want to just live our lives, you know? I want my parents off my back, and I want school to just go away until I'm interested in it again." He ran his hand along his buzz cut, a little bit of comfort in the velvet. "It just seems so useless now. Like stalling."

I must admit, I'd been having the same thoughts all week. There had been a time when I'd felt like I was learning something new every day, when I'd felt like I was getting things done instead of waiting to be ready to get things done. That time had been long ago.

"Well," I said, "we could just do that."

"Do what?"

"Move forward. Pause school again, until we're ready, but move everything else up. Buy a house. Get married. Start making life happen."

He looked at me like I'd sprouted an extra ear. "You think we're ready for that?"

"We've got decent jobs, and we've got a little bit of savings. Renting is a sucker's game, you've always said. So? Why not?"

"Let me think about it."

So, I went back to my textbook and promptly fell asleep with my nose in the spine, and he went back to contemplating the ceiling. It took another frustrating school day for him to sit down next to me and finally say, "Okay. Let's do it."

We celebrated that night with sparkling wine and pizza, and the next day, instead of going to class, we went house hunting, and started wedding planning.

There weren't a lot of houses in our price range—we were really looking for something that on a good day would pass as a starter home—but eventually we found a couple of landed trailers in the foothills and started talking to realtors.

Then we looked up local Lutheran churches, and picked one that we had been to before. We were working all the time, so we hadn't been going to church, but when we did go, this one seemed welcoming.

Pastor Hank stood up from his desk to greet us. "Jake and Heidi, was it?"

We murmured our thanks as we took seats across from him. We were both dressed in our Sunday best. Jake looked trim and dapper, and I wore something pretty and demure, something that screamed *Wife Material* from the rooftops. His office was full of knickknacks—miniature crosses and statues of shepherds—and there were several different translations of the Bible spread across his desk. It looked like everything I expected a pastor's office to look like.

"So," he began, "what can I do for you?"

Jake looked at me, so I started. "Well, we're recently engaged," I flashed my gorgeous ring at him for a moment, "and I guess we're looking for a church to get married in."

Pastor Hank smiled, the slow, satisfied smile of someone practiced in having all the answers. "That sounds wonderful. I should warn you, I'm not a wedding planner. I'm just an officiant."

"We were thinking it would be quite a small wedding," Jake said. "We don't need much."

"Of course. Shall we make a start?" We nodded, and he carried on. "The first thing I usually talk about with new couples is the importance of marriage counseling before the wedding. I can't stress that step enough. Marriage is a holy rite before God, and you must not enter into it lightly."

"Naturally," I said, and nodded with conviction. Jake let his hand drop into mine, and I gave it a reassuring squeeze.

Pastor Hank was pressing on. "I usually try to match the scriptures I read to the personalities of the couple, though I'd want to include the old standbys as well: 'Love is patient, love is kind,' and so on. Do you have any scriptures you're particularly attached to?"

While both of us were spiritual and had been raised with a deep faith, memorizing scripture was not in our DNA. We made a few noncommittal noises. We hadn't even considered scripture. We'd just figured that to get married, you go get a pastor, and everything sort of works out.

"Well, you've got time to work that out."

We nodded again. Truth be told, this interview was becoming kind of overwhelming. We'd both grown up going to church and had expectations of being married in a church.

As a kid growing up you went, you put money in the plate, you bowed your head and sang a few hymns, and then you went down to the basement and ate cookies as your parents connected with their friends. There wasn't anything about this church that felt like it was ours, and it was feeling less and less like home by the moment.

"I've got one last question," the pastor began. "And it's a little delicate. How much . . . time . . . do you spend together?"

What did this question mean? Was he asking how much time we spent having sex? Could he do that? Jake and I looked at each other. We were in a church, talking to a pastor. We couldn't lie to him. That probably counted as a double sin. I squeezed Jake's hand again. "Actually, Pastor Hank," Jake said, "we've been living together for several months now."

"Ah," said Pastor Hank, sitting back in his chair. He steepled his fingers and looked dreadfully disappointed. "That's a problem."

"Why?" Jake and I spoke in unison.

Pastor Hank sucked in a breath, as if he were about to tell us a terrible truth. "The thing is, kids, we're really looking to foster healthy marriages. I can't give my church's seal of approval for a marriage that has an inherently unhealthy beginning."

"Excuse me?" I said, leaning forward. Pastor Hank visibly shrank away from me, as if I were diseased.

"It's nothing personal, you understand," he said, standing up and stepping away from his desk. "But the church is against cohabitation and promiscuity before marriage."

"You'd rather we continued to live in sin than be married?" Jake's voice was incredulous. I couldn't believe it either.

"If you two were willing to separate for a time, and then perhaps come back to me, perhaps I could help you, but without that, I'm not sure there'd be any evidence that would make me believe your decision was sincere. And I can't marry a couple whose devotion I doubt."

I stood up so quickly that my chair scooted back behind, a nasty retort ready on my tongue. And then I thought better of it. "Okay," I said, willing my voice to be cheerful. "Thank you for being so upfront with us. Let's go, Jake." As we left the office, I shared a glance with Jake. We both understood where the pastor was coming from. We had both been raised with those same values. But in my heart, we were already married. We were just looking to make it official with some paperwork and a service before God. Why couldn't the pastor understand that?

We walked—our pace slow and deeply dignified—out to our car, and we drove home to the apartment we shared. Excuse me, "cohabitated."

When we got there, we sat in the car in the driveway.

"Can you believe that guy?" asked Jake.

"Yeah. You'd think he'd be a little more concerned with the spiritual well-being of his flock."

"I guess we're never going back there."

"Nope."

Plan B was the justice of the peace. They had zero qualms about marrying us, regardless of our living situation. And, as a bonus, it turned out that a courthouse wedding only cost around twenty-five dollars. We were sold, and we pulled a date out of midair: November 4, 2002.

It turned out that my family couldn't make it (hard to get off work for a Monday wedding), and we didn't really mind that much. It wasn't like we were putting on a show or eager to feed everyone. We didn't feel like our marriage had anything to do with anyone else. What could be more intimate than a vow you make to only one person? It wasn't traditional, but we were fiercely independent. Being married, even if it was just the two of us, was the only thing that mattered to us.

November 4, 2002, was a chilly, cloudy day in Albuquerque. We both had to work, but we'd made sure that we could clock out before the courthouse closed. I spent my whole shift daydreaming about what was to come. I clocked out on time, 3:00 p.m. sharp, and got home with enough time to shimmy into my ivory, tight-fitting, sleeveless dress, the one that went to just above my knees (it happened to be the same dress I wore the night Jake proposed). I was never going to be one of those brides who fell into rhapsodies about all the tulle and lace on her dress. I liked the dress I wore, and really, that was all that mattered to me. Getting married isn't about how you look, it's about joining together, forever, for real.

At 3:45, Jake stepped into the bedroom, clearing his throat pointedly and checking his watch. "I know, I know," I said, still fiddling with my hair. "Five minutes." It was a strange moment—I was all about eschewing traditional wedding craziness, but as we neared the "I do" moment, I found myself wishing I had a little more time to primp. After all, I'd cared about looking great when Jake proposed, and that was exactly as private as the wedding was going to be.

89

"Yeah," Jake said, "but you said that five minutes ago. Courthouse closes at five. You want to get married today?"

I huffed at the mirror, exasperated. Jake managed to look great without even trying—all he had to do was throw on a suit and he looked like James Bond. "Fine," I said, and forced myself to put down the brush. "I'm good. We're good."

Jake held the door open as I pushed past him. "You're beautiful," he said.

Even today, every moment of that rush to the courthouse feels distinct. The clunk of my heels on the concrete. The smell of the dust that had accumulated on Jake's suit. The vibrant yellows of the blooming acacia tree over our front walk. The strength of Jake's hand in mine. Everything was coming together, humming: *Today Is the Day!*

Nothing, not my stress over my hair, not our worries about getting there on time, not even the clouds that hung dark and heavy in the sky, could spoil that fact. It was happening.

"Which shop did your mom talk to?" Jake asked, as the car pulled into traffic.

"Lilah's Flowers," I said, "It's on Mariposa, I think."

Jake shook his head. "It can't be," he said. "That's on the wrong side of town. We'd have to go a couple miles past the courthouse to get to it."

I grabbed my purse and fished around until I found the printout of my mom's email. "Shit," I said. "It's definitely Lilah's Flowers."

Jake took a deep breath, his eyes on the car's clock.

"It's okay," I said. "I don't need a bouquet. It's fine."

He glanced over at me—at my fancy-but-not-wedding-fancy dress, at my almost finished hair, at the email printout that represented the whole of my family present that day—and then he glanced at the clock. "We can make it," he said, and pressed his foot to the gas.

And that was when the sky opened up, and what felt like a whole lake fell on top of us. The rain made everything slower. New Mexico drivers don't see a lot of rain, so it takes them a minute to adjust—plus everyone is afraid of oil slicks in the road—but Jake is a Chicago boy. He knows how to drive in the rain. The challenge was just dealing with the other drivers. And now we were trying to speed.

I gripped the panic handle as he wove in and out of traffic, sailing through yellow lights and nipping past pedestrians who cowered under newspapers when they should have been watching the road. We got to Lilah's Flowers just as the clock turned over to 4:23, and we leapt out into the rain. I had Jake's suit jacket stretched over my head to protect my hair, but I'm not sure it did much good.

Luckily, Lilah's Flowers had the bouquet all prepared. My mother had called in an order a week earlier, and the florist was waiting for us. "Cutting it a little close, aren't you?" she said, as she passed the flowers over the desk. Roses and lilies, in varying shades of lilac and peach. It was lovely, but we didn't have enough time to really appreciate it. Bouquet in hand, we raced back to the car, and then back into traffic.

When we finally arrived at the courthouse, splashing through puddles to get in, it looked like it had already closed. Not a person in sight.

We ran up the stairs to the correct room and found our judge: a little old man with oversized coke-bottle lenses. He helped us through the paperwork and then started looking around, as if there were supposed to be more people. And then he asked about witnesses.

That was when we panicked.

At the last National Guard drill, we'd hit it off with a new girl—we were never able to remember her first name, so we'd just called her Clark—and because we got along so well, we'd asked her to come be our witness. And then we'd forgotten about it completely. We hadn't called to remind her or anything, and she didn't seem to be in the courthouse that day. We were screwed.

Jake and I looked at each other with dismay. If we didn't have a witness, we wouldn't be able to get married. All this rushing around and stressing out, for nothing. And we wanted this marriage so badly. This was supposed to be The Day.

But here's the truth. No matter what comes, there was no problem that Jake and I couldn't solve if we worked together. We took a step away from the judge and went into a football huddle. "Okay," Jake said, "There's no way we're leaving here without becoming Mr. and Mrs. Radkiewicz. That's just not happening."

I nodded. "Time for Plan B."

"Exactly. There's got to be someone else in this building who can come be a witness."

"Anybody else," I said. "You want to split up and go witness hunting?"

"Just what I was going to say," and he leaned in and kissed me. "Sometimes, it's like we have the same brain."

I grinned, and we straightened up. With that, the little judge watched bemusedly as we took off—each in a separate direction—looking for anybody in the building who might agree to be our witness. We met up back on the ground floor, where two older, friendly looking Latina ladies were mopping the floor. "Excuse me!" I said, waving my bouquet in explanation, "Could you possibly witness our wedding?"

The ladies looked at me, uncomprehending. "Sí. No habla inglés," one of them said.

What followed must have been the most ridiculous show these ladies had ever seen, as Jake and I tried to explain witnessing a wedding through mime. I found myself wishing I had paid more attention in Mrs. Jones's high school Spanish class. At some point, they just started giggling. We took that as agreement and rushed back up the stairs, trying to cajole our new witnesses to greater speeds as we went.

The judge was still there, thank goodness, and said we could proceed. We were holding each other's hands, about to begin the ceremony, when Clark strolled in, colossally late but unconcerned. She'd brought a camera, which we'd completely forgotten, so everything was forgiven. She set about taking pictures of us, the judge, the witnesses, my mom's bouquet, everything. We ended up being so grateful for those photos. Memory can be strong, but it's never as solid as you think.

I started crying as soon as the ceremony began. Uncontrollable tears, my body shaking with sobs—I'd never felt emotion that powerful before. I was somehow able to push out the words necessary to complete my vows: "I, Heidi, choose you, Jacob, to be my loving husband. I promise before God and our friends and loved ones to love and honor you, and to protect and keep you, in sickness and in health, in joy and in sorrow, in times of peace and in times of hardship; and, forsaking all others, I will cherish you alone above all others in the world to walk by my side and to be in my heart as my loving husband, the love of my life, and the sunlight of my heart, all the days of my life!" That's when I noticed that Jake was tearing up as well, which set me off all over again.

I glanced over as the judge was offering his final few words, and saw that our lovely, giggling witnesses were also crying their eyes out. Everyone had lost it. We could have used their mops for tissues.

All in all, we got what we wanted out of the day. Maybe my family couldn't be there with us, but that just meant that we could focus on each other. And miraculously, we had pictures to show everyone later.

The courthouse was locking up as we left, and even though the rain hadn't let up, we felt like we were flying. You ever have a day where you step outside and the colors around you all seem brighter? The leaves on the trees are greener than you thought possible, and the flowers in the hedgerows seem like they're exploding with color? Birdsong is sweeter, and the wind almost smells perfumed?

This was like that, times a thousand.

Our hearts were singing. Our skin was buzzing. We were lighter than air. The rain didn't feel cold—it felt romantic and mysterious. The rush we'd been through didn't feel stressful any more—it felt like a challenge that we'd conquered. The fact that we hadn't had our family there didn't feel sad—it felt intimate and exciting, like our love was forbidden, and we'd had to cross mountains and battle monsters to be together.

That evening, as we slid into the car, we knew that we were warriors. I looked over at Jake, and he looked over at me, and together we said, "We're married." The words felt strange and new as they rolled off our tongues.

There was only one thing left to decide:

"Dinner?" Jake had started the car and pulled out on the main road.

I giggled and corrected him. "Our *reception* dinner," I said. "Where do you want to go?"

"I dunno," I said, leaning back into my seat, more relaxed than I'd been in months. I was Mrs. Radkiewicz now. I was a wife. I had a husband. Other things mattered, of course, but nothing mattered *more*.

"Well, I'm hungry," said Jake, "so let's make a plan. How do you feel about El Pinto?"

"Eh. I don't feel like Mexican."

"Chinese?"

That was when I saw the perfect place. "There!" I shouted, jabbing my finger against the car window. "That place!"

Jake looked, and sighed. "The Macaroni Grill?" he said. "Really?"

"Yesssssss," I said, suddenly salivating at the thought of pasta and cheese and garlic bread.

Jake grimaced. As a native Chicagoan, he had high—some (not me, obviously) might say ridiculously high—standards when it came to Italian food. "You don't want to go somewhere nicer, maybe? It's our reception dinner, after all."

"Nope." I was dead set. This was what I wanted, and he knew better than to try to dissuade me.

"Okay," he said, and steered the car into the Macaroni Grill parking lot.

When we walked in, I felt certain that there was some sort of just-married glow that we gave off, because it felt like everyone in the restaurant knew that we were married. No one said anything, of course, but I could feel that they knew.

We didn't get dessert. There was ice cream at home, and considering this was our wedding night, I had some creative ideas for its use. Afterwards, I fell asleep in the arms of my husband, confident that everything was right in the world.

I learned a month later that Jake hadn't told his family about the wedding. They didn't even know that we'd gotten engaged, much less married. I wasn't fully sure how I felt about him not telling them. On the one hand, I just wanted to be with him, and why should I care about their approval? But, on the other hand, I knew how our sudden-seeming wedding would look to them. Their first assumption would be that I was knocked up. That our marriage was just a smoke screen for a rash decision, and that we hadn't really thought it all through. That thought hurt.

"Okay," he said, after I'd explained my anxieties to him. And he picked up the telephone, "I guess I'd better tell them."

And I smiled, and braced for impact.

CHAPTER 8

Gathering Storm Clouds

Two months of wedded bliss had passed in a sort of happy fog, where even the most mundane of tasks felt glittery and meaningful. But one Monday, after drill, we were home, putting away the week's groceries, when the phone rang. I was trying to find space in the fridge for an oversized bunch of celery, so Jake got to it first. I wasn't listening at first, but my ears perked up when his tone dropped. "We are?" Jake sounded surprised. He then asked two questions in quick succession: "When will this happen? What do we need to do?" He was quiet for a long time, listening, before saying, "Okay, we'll be there," and hanging up the phone.

"Jake, who was that?" I wanted to believe it was our realtor with a place for us to look at, but I'd heard the rumors. I think, somewhere in the pit of my stomach, I knew who'd been on the other end of the line. "What's going on?"

"They want us back at drill this weekend. They'll tell us then."

Deployment. Son of a bitch, it was finally happening. I'd known it would only be a matter of time, but I'd gotten caught up in life. Work. Romance. Our wedding. Trying to buy a house. Everything had been going so nicely. I should have known something like this would happen.

We called our families to let them know that the day had come. Everyone promised to come down next weekend, to take the time to say goodbye.

My nerves that week were off the charts. I kept imagining car bombs and bullets whizzing past and wondering what if one of us got injured? Or *died*? Bleeding into the sand, fingers twitching from misfiring nerves—the grisly images, all figments of Hollywood creations and my own overactive imagination, played on repeat behind my eyelids.

When the morning came, Jake and I put on our uniforms in silence. I couldn't tell what he was feeling—but could feel both anxiety and excitement vying for my attention. This was what I'd wanted. I'd wanted to fight after 9/11. I'd wanted my revenge on those terrorist bastards. I was about to head out the bedroom door when Jake snagged my hand and pulled me back into a tight bear hug.

"You okay?" he asked.

"Kind of," I said. My voice was muffled against the rough canvas of his uniform.

"No matter what happens," he said, his breath hot in my ear, "we'll deal with it together."

That morning at drill, formation was slow to start. The air was tense with anxiety and concern for what was probably going to happen. Everyone had a life here. Everyone had expected this day to come, but we'd all expected it would come at some unspecified future—*someday* it'll happen, but it couldn't possibly happen *now*. But it was. It was happening *now*.

We all milled around the armory, talking quietly amongst ourselves, waiting for the official word. The lieutenant arrived, and we hustled into formation, and it was then that he pronounced our fate. "We have been given orders to go to Fort Bliss, Texas, and begin training. You've got one week from today before you're on active duty. When you go home this weekend, start squaring things away with your jobs and homes. You're gonna be gone for a while."

One week to put our lives in storage. One week to say goodbye to our families. One week to spend with our fur babies. One week until the inevitable. It didn't seem reasonable. I wanted to grab Jake's hand, to reassure him as I reassured myself. At least we were together.

But when formation ended, our lieutenant pulled both of us into his office. We stood at ease as he leaned into his knuckles on his desk, his face worried and pinched. "I want you two to know that I hate this," he said. "But Jake isn't an 88Mike," (that's a truck driver), "and we don't have the time to train him. He won't be shipping out with our unit."

I broke my stance, put a hand on Jake's shoulder. I thought I might faint. The words practically spilling out of my mouth, I said, "But, but, he's trained for running construction equipment. Isn't that good enough?"

"It's not," he said, and he looked genuinely sorry about it. "I'm afraid you'll be going without him, Heidi."

It was as if the world had come crashing down upon me; as if my soul had been ripped out of my body and crushed. I couldn't breathe. It felt as if someone had shoved their fist into my stomach and then kept going. My mind went blank, save for one deafening thought: My husband is not coming with me. *My husband is not coming with me.* MY HUSBAND IS NOT COMING WITH ME.

I must have been hyperventilating, because when I looked up, Jake was propping me up by both shoulders and the lieutenant had taken a couple of concerned steps closer. "There's one thing you guys can do to assure that you both stay stateside," he said.

"What do you mean?" The confusion in Jake's voice surprised us both.

"Your only option," said the Lieutenant, "is for Heidi to get pregnant."

We blinked at him for a second. Pregnant? What? We'd been married a month. We'd been together for a year. Have a baby? Really? I didn't even like to babysit.

"LT, thanks for the very candid advice, but we both want to go" I said. "I mean, we really want to go. It's what we trained for all these years, and after 9/11, it just seems right."

The lieutenant nodded sadly. "I wish I could help, I really do. I just don't see any other way."

And then we had a decidedly strange moment. A strange, glowing moment of stress and fear, in which the bond that had pulled us together hummed with—I don't want to call

100

it a telepathic link, but it may as well have been—born of experience and the certainty that we knew each other, inside and out. A moment where all of the things we'd known we'd wanted for the future—home, family, stability—were suddenly rushing toward us. We wanted all these things, but we wanted them after we'd had the chance to serve our country, together. We had been waiting for this day since 9/11, and we still wanted our chance to do something. But it was all going terribly wrong.

We took our leave of the lieutenant, both of us quiet over this new, unspoken possibility, still in a bit of shock.

We left the drill hall, not saying a word. Jake got in the driver's seat, closed the door wordlessly, and drove. I sat back in my seat and watched as the telephone poles lining the interstate blipped past. I thought about my parents and my childhood, and what I wanted for my children—how I wanted so much for them, and how, right now, I wasn't ready to give it to them. The future was so uncertain. We'd only just gotten our lives together. We'd thought we were so grown-up—married and trying to buy a house and so happy that it ached—but now . . . who knew where we'd be in a year? Our lives together could be ripped apart in the space of a week. I don't think I noticed the way my chest grew tight, or how my breath started coming in gasps. I just know that I felt Jake's hand in mine, and I realized that I was sobbing.

"Jake," I said, through the sobs, "can we make a stop before we get home?" My family was all there. I couldn't imagine what we would tell them.

"Of course," he said. "Where?"

I just needed some time. "I don't know. Somewhere where we can think. And pray."

Jake saw a sign up ahead. "How about the hospital? They should have a chapel."

"Okay," I said. It felt like fate.

We walked straight in, following the signs on the ceiling, hand-in-hand. A tiny alcove off to the side, the chapel was clean and still and quiet. A little picture of Jesus hung on the far wall, but otherwise, it was a simple room. A place whose only purpose was to let you be alone with God, to bring him your problems, and to let your mind be still enough to hear his answers.

I'd spent my childhood going to church every Sunday, but this was different. I'd never needed God more than I did right now. We took a pew together, held each other, and let the stress of the day roll through us. Both of us wept, great heaving sobs that left our bodies aching, as though our fear and grief could flow out of us through the tears. When I could finally speak, I prayed aloud. "God, I've never really asked you for much, but please let Jake go with me overseas. We need to be together. Whatever happens, don't let us be apart."

My whole family was waiting for us when we got home. From the moment we walked in, they could see from my face that something was terribly wrong. My face was beet red and splotchy. A dried-up crust of salt and tears had formed along my eyes. Jake had to break the news: "We were told that I wouldn't be able to go overseas with Heidi."

They gaped at us. "Wouldn't they rather have Jake go over, instead?" my dad asked, but I was too upset to register the insult. My mom, stepmom, and sister all burst into tears. We huddled together, one big group hug that shuddered and sniffled.

I looked up after a while and said, "The LT did mention one possibility." My parents' eyes lit up, everyone hanging on to what I would say next.

"What?" My sister was rubbing at her eyes. "Tell us, what do you mean?"

I choked a little on my words. "He said . . ." I hesitated, not sure this was an option that Jake and I had completely thought through. "He said that if I were pregnant they couldn't send me." My parents all looked bewildered at the idea, and then my dad made a totally uncharacteristic statement: "Then I guess it's time for you two to go make a baby."

My head popped up. Had he really just said that? Because of him, I'd spent my entire adolescence pretending that female anatomy wasn't even real, and now he wanted me to go off and "make a baby?" Our group cry dried up as everyone tried to make sense of this new development. My sister and I, shocked beyond words, had one of those psychic moments that you only get from decades of sisterly coexistence. Had our father just suggested going off and having sex?

"I'm not kidding," he said to me, a smug smile playing around his face. He was watching me struggle to reconcile the man I'd grown up with and this new, weirdly explicit man in my living room. "Really. We'll watch a movie or something. You and Jake should go . . . do your thing."

"No way," I said. "There is no way this is happening with all of you in the apartment, and it is DEFINITELY not happening while you're in the living room."

I looked at Jake as they gathered their things and headed for the door. Was this what we really wanted? I knew that we'd wanted this in the future, but it was all happening so fast. As the door closed behind them Jake and I sat still in the quiet apartment, overwhelmed by the rush of thoughts and emotions, until we realized that we'd been staring blankly at each other. This was a one-way road. If we made this decision, that was it.

Finally, Jake, his voice quiet, said, "We were praying for a miracle."

I tilted my head, not quite understanding.

A slight smile crept onto his face. "Your dad, telling us to go make a baby, and your mom agreeing, I think that counts." I giggled. Twenty-two years of complete silence on the subject, and now they talk about it.

"Do you think we're ready for this?" I asked.

"I think that whatever happens, as long we are together, we will be happy."

"What about our duty to this country?"

He shrugged. "Our first choice is that we both go, but the truth is that pregnancy isn't really up to us. We can try, but ultimately, it's in God's hands."

The next morning, Jake got a phone call from our lieutenant. I sat across the kitchen table from him as he spoke, my fingernails chewed to bits, listening for clues to our fate. "Are you serious?" he asked, excitement building in his voice. "Are you sure about that? Thank you so much, sir!"

I watched him hang up the phone, counting the moments until I had his attention again. "So?"

"The lieutenant says I will be going, after all!"

"What?" I said, bowled over.

"LT said that there weren't enough people on the roster to fill all the positions needed, and I don't need to do the training to become an 88M!"

It had been a tumultuous week, with me riding the line between crying/not-crying pretty hard, so it wasn't surprising when I burst into tears again, this time in elation. God had heard our prayers. He'd answered us, and made our way together safe and solid. I felt like yesterday's desperation had awakened a faith that I hadn't even known I was missing. God is real, and he wanted Jake and me to be together.

When I could finally breathe again, I was in Jake's arms. My family was gathered around us, everyone in one stage or another of shock or joy. My dad was grinning. "And to think," he said, "last night, you guys were trying to make a baby."

And it hit home. If I was pregnant, Jake would be overseas without me, and we'd be in the same awful mess, just in reverse. I pulled Jake into the bathroom and closed the door. "What do we do? About the maybe-baby?"

"You probably aren't pregnant," he said. But neither of us could know that.

"I want babies," I said. "But not right now. Not just when we're heading off to serve our country."

"I know," said Jake. "Me too. But listen, Heidi. God cleared the way for us to be together many times. You've got to have faith that He's going to keep us both on this path. He wants us together."

I did have faith, but sometimes, when you're faced with challenges, it can be difficult to stay strong. That first rush of certainty was already fading. But I also knew that I didn't have much in the way of options. Either I was pregnant, and I'd come home just as Jake was shipping out, or I wasn't, and we'd ship out together. And in the end, both of those options sounded good to me. I knew which one I'd prefer—sticking by my husband and serving my country—but I also knew that I'd be happy with a baby. Everything was going to be okay. Even if I didn't necessarily have faith that God's plans perfectly matched mine, I was sure that no matter what happened, Jake and I would find the good in it.

My family helped us pack up our lives and fit them into storage, and then we made our tearful goodbyes. There's only so much bluster a person can manage in that situation. In the back of my mind, I wondered if I would ever see them again. I was only just coming to grips with the idea that I was going to war. I promised I would write to them, and I squeezed my mom, dad, stepmom, stepdad, and sister so hard that I was sure they were going to pop.

Jake's family arrived almost as soon as my family had left. Jake had only told them about our wedding a month or so ago, but the stress of our deployment appeared to have displaced any lingering resentment in their minds. They were happy to see us, and they took us out to dinner that night. As we talked, I wondered how long it would last, this newfound friendliness, and whether Jake had needed to be deployed to win their approval. But I didn't think about it for too long. I finally felt like part of the family, and I wasn't about to screw it up by overthinking.

That next morning, we said our goodbyes to his parents and our dogs. We've always coddled the dogs (they were our babies, after all), so saying goodbye was wrenching. The dogs couldn't know what was happening or that their lives would soon be turned upside down, but Jake's parents agreed to take them back home with them, to Chicago, and keep them until we get back. It didn't make saying goodbye to them any easier. We must have sat there for an hour, petting our boys and loving on them as much as we could. I think that was the hardest goodbye. It was certainly the goodbye we cried the hardest for.

Saying goodbye to the in-laws was a little easier. Visiting with them had been nice, but it still wasn't perfect. Maybe a few months of deployment would soften things to the point where I could feel like a proper daughter to them. "Thank you," I said, finally, "thank you for everything."

I think I spotted a few tears in my mother-in-law's eyes. "We wouldn't do it any other way. It's the least we can do."

CHAPTER 9

A Vision of Things to Come

*C*amp *Cedar, August 2003.*

Between the tents, someone is shouting. The alleys between tents are shaded and breezy, which makes them a popular hangout spot for anyone trying to escape the desert heat, but as I duck under the overhang, I discover someone putting them to a new use. SPC Sven hunches over Quintariz, whose face is a grimace of pain. A few other soldiers are crowded around them, wincing and groaning in sync with Quintariz.

"Hold still!" Sven says. "If you move, it's gonna look funny."

I peek over the huddle of soldiers. With what looks and sounds like a tattoo gun, Sven is etching something on Quintariz's arm.

I clap a hand over my mouth. Tattoos in the middle of the desert, in somewhat less than sterile conditions. I shouldn't have been surprised. At least these guys had found a way to beat the heat and boredom. "How clean is that?" I ask, "and when were we issued a tattoo gun?"

"You up next, Radkiewicz?" Sven asks, glancing up at me.

"Argh, damnit!" Quintariz yelps as Sven's needle goes a little off course and a little too deep.

"And get some kind of Middle Eastern flesh-eating bacteria permanently inked into my arm?" I say, watching as Sven puts the finishing touches on the insignia. "I think I'll pass."

Sven grins, and reaches for a bandage. "Your loss," he says.

"Seriously, though—where'd you get the tattoo gun?" I ask, my curiosity getting the best of me.

"I made it," he begins, "from an old hair trimmer. I got a pen for the ink and a paper clip for the needle."

I laugh, and the guys around me laugh too. "Yeah, that sounds way too close to prison style for me."

* * *

Deployment was a long process, but when my period showed up to assure me that our baby-making efforts had failed, I was relieved. It only reinforced my faith that God was looking out for us.

We first reported to the guard unit in Las Vegas, New Mexico, which seemed to be as far from anything interesting as the dark side of the moon. Perched seven thousand feet above sea level in the southern Rockies, every day of the two weeks we spent there was cold, dull, and wet. We were there only to pack up our unit's gear and fill out paperwork.

We had only been part of this unit for a few months and didn't really know many of the other soldiers well. Those two weeks were great for getting better acquainted with some of our new battle buddies before shipping out. From mail carriers and police officers to tattoo artists and petty schemers, our unit was well-stocked with men and women eager to bring the fight to the enemy.

Our eventual location was still a mystery and the subject of endless rumors, but the assumption was that we would be going to the sandbox (army slang for somewhere in the Middle East) in some capacity. Probably a toss-up between Iraq and Afghanistan, but no one was sure. All we knew was that our unit had been activated and we had orders for six months.

After Las Vegas, we got orders to head down to Fort Bliss, in El Paso, Texas. That would be our final training base before shipping out. When we left, we were quite a sight. The rest of our unit's friends and family lined up along the side of the road, complete with signs and bullhorns, to give us a proper send-off. We were in seventy or so 915 semi-truck/trailers, all set to barrel down the New Mexico highway. Jake and I ended up in separate trucks, but we were heading to the same place. I felt pumped and excited. I'd never been further south than Albuquerque.

I was really taken with Fort Bliss's name. I imagined perfect weather, some palm trees, and lush green hills. There can be only one reason why the base was named Fort Bliss. Surely it must be blissful. I was sadly mistaken. Military bases are all pretty much the same. Lots of brick buildings, concrete, and landscaping going brown and dry in the heat. Fort not-so-Bliss wasn't any different.

We parked our trucks outside of a giant brick auditorium and headed inside, where what seemed like thousands of other soldiers were listening to an officer lecture from a stage up front. I didn't listen very closely; it was mostly the same rules and regulations you find on other bases, with a minor difference in that the border was just a few miles south. He wanted us to be careful about getting too close.

We were eventually assigned to a barracks that looked a lot like a college dorm, and after a minute or two of getting acquainted with our roommates, we were shown to our mess hall: a wooden building that showed its age and served terrible prepackaged glop in place of actual food. This was the moment when all the excitement and fanfare faded away and reality settled in. Our entire world was changing. We were now active duty soldiers stationed on an army base. Our civilian mindset was about to be dramatically upturned.

The military sets your life up in such a way that you're not supposed to have time to feel lonesome. You're not supposed to have a moment free to ruminate on what you're giving up and who you wish was with you. But lying in our beds at night, it was easy to remember our favorite restaurants, and what it felt like to have a Sunday afternoon free. Leisurely afternoon lovemaking, punctuated by naps and laughter, was a thing of the past. We had no idea when we'd next get to feel that kind of ease.

Health prep was a big part of deploying overseas. The army knew exactly what kind of exotic diseases we were likely to encounter, so the medics had a long list of inoculations. As I watched the medic prepare all of the syringes, I counted one, two, three. I kept counting till seven.

"What are all those for?" I asked as he laid them out before me. "They can't all be for me?"

"They sure are," he said. "This one is a flu shot, this one is for tetanus . . ." I listened as he listed a few diseases I was familiar with. Then he got to "anthrax, smallpox, and Japanese encephalitis." And I got kind of nervous. "The anthrax one is going to hurt a little, but the rest shouldn't be that bad."

He was right. The anthrax shot had a bit of a sting and it left a big cold lump of something under the skin that we had to massage in. As we all stood around rubbing the cold lump on our shoulders, we were briefed about the possibility of being attacked with a biological weapon—hence the anthrax and smallpox vaccines. All very reassuring.

The rest of our time was devoted to refresher courses and gear maintenance. We spent a lot of time "taking inventory" of all the equipment on our trucks. The higher ups usually budgeted half a day for inventory, but we never needed all that time. We'd usually finish after a couple hours and spend the rest of the time wandering around the motor pool, looking for a good place to nap.

After a solid month of nonstop training, we started getting leave on some of the weekends. Some of the guys sneaked out to cross the border and see what trouble they could find in Juarez, but Jake, Skinny, and I ended up spending a lot of time at the tattoo parlor. SGT Brujillo (we called him Skinny) was a soft-spoken guy who must have had the military in his DNA. He had worked as a mechanic back in civilian life, and I never understood why he didn't make the army his career. His sense of humor was just a little bit dryer than the climate we were in, and Jake and I became best of friends with him.

I'd always wanted a tattoo, but Jake wasn't a fan. He objected to pretty much all of my ideas. He thought if I got one, he would wake up one day to find me covered in them. And that's okay, I knew that wasn't going to happen. I heard him out, making sure that I gave him enough space to truly articulate his argument, and I considered his points carefully. In the end, he came with me.

I opted for something pretty and feminine, choosing a design of a hummingbird flying next to flowers, and decided to put it on my lower back, so it would be visible whenever I wore something midriff-baring. Thinking about it there made me feel a little rebellious and sexy, like I was decorating myself with secret, hidden art. The process of getting it was anything but hot, though. The minute the tattoo artist started in with the needle, I let loose with a string of profanity that I didn't even know was in me. I'm telling you, I put sailors to shame. The tattoo artist even asked me if I wanted him to stop—apparently I was scaring away potential customers. I shut up, and I didn't ask him to stop. Eventually the pain became bearable, and I emerged, adorned with fresh ink and a feeling of invincibility.

I don't know how it happened, but after watching me go through the tattoo process, Jake reversed his earlier all-tattoos-are-evil stance and decided to get one for himself. His was a picture of an eagle breaking through the skin, with the words "US Army" on his upper bicep. It was damn hot. Together, we looked fierce. Ready for the war. (Who wouldn't be afraid of a little blonde girl with a rifle and a *magnificent* hummingbird tattoo?)

The hardest part of army life is dealing with boredom. I won't deny that combat is dangerous and terrifying, but at least it gives you something to focus on. Before we shipped out, we got our first real taste of the kind of boredom waiting for us. One weekend, midway through our second month, our company was given the responsibility of guarding the ammunition depot over the weekend. It wasn't a big job, requiring just a couple soldiers to carry out, but it did mean that whoever did it wouldn't have the weekend to go off and see family, and any weekend could be the last chance to see family. Our family was nowhere nearby, so Jake and I took that bullet.

We drove out to the site, two rickety shacks out in a desolate spot of desert, surrounded by sand and tumbleweed and miles of empty horizon. Strictly speaking, "guarding" doesn't actually require you to stand at attention for hours on end, constantly scanning the landscape for trouble. This was an ammo depot in the middle of Texas. No one was going to attack it. No one was even going to show up to check on us. We had a weekend of unsupervised solitude. You can guess how we used our time. They let a married couple go on a weekend-long duty together, unsupervised, and our unauthorized activities just made us that much more vigilant about unwanted guests.

Despite the boredom, those two months were great for us. You know how fulfilling it is when you get to spend all your time doing the work that you love, that uses all your strengths and makes you happy to get up in the morning? And doing it alongside your best friend and lover amplifies that satisfaction tenfold? Yeah, we didn't do any of that kind of work. It was a lot of stalling and make-work, designed to keep us busy and amp up the crazy in us to the point where we wanted to go to war. But it was still great fun and we were starting to feel at home with our new unit.

Our last week at Fort Bliss was full of reinforcing training exercises. We went through another gas chamber exercise, just to hammer home the idea that being gassed would be really awful, but honestly, in the time it takes to don your NBC (nuclear, biological, chemical) gear—lots of little pieces and straps and fiddly bits—you've probably already been gassed to death. Best to just pray that the enemy keeps his hands off the biological and chemical weapons.

On March 19, 2003, we were out in the southern desert of Texas, covered in dust and sand, lining up the trucks in a herringbone formation—the sort that would soon become all too familiar—when Jake brought out his pocket radio.

"The President's about to speak." Jake said, and everyone got quiet and huddled in closer.

From the radio, there was the familiar crackle as President Bush took the microphone. "My fellow citizens," he began, "at this hour, American and coalition forces are in the early stages of military operations to disarm Iraq, to free its people, and to defend the world from grave danger. . ."

Everyone in our huddle celebrated, and the weight of the moment sunk in. We were going, no doubt about it now. I know—no one should celebrate a war—but the fact is that when you've trained for something and are finally given the opportunity to use that training, you're going to be excited.

Leave the moral questions about peace and protectionism to Congress. We were all eager to get overseas. This was what we'd been waiting for. We were all warriors.

CHAPTER 10

Stop and Start

April 21, 2003. Fort Bliss, Texas.

My alarm went off at 3:00 a.m. We'd packed the night before, so when I rolled out of my barracks bed, all of my gear was piled neatly at the foot, waiting for me. Everything I'd need for the foreseeable future was sealed in Ziploc bags and tidily stowed in a rucksack, a civilian backpack, and two duffle bags. (They never did tell us why we had to use the Ziplocs. Theories ranged from "magical space-saving vacuum bag" to "it'll keep our stuff dry if the plane crashes into the ocean," though at that point, we were pretty sure no one would give two shits about soggy socks and underwear.)

I needed two trips to bring all of my stuff down to the formation area, stacking and spacing it neatly, as if it were standing in formation next to us. No one knew why we had to be out here so early. The sun wasn't even up yet. Once everyone had their gear staged, we were forbidden to go back and mess with it. We had to stand around, waiting for the MPs. When they finally arrived, they came with dogs and trucks, and they carefully led the dogs from pile to pile. Searching for bombs or drugs, we guessed, though the irony of our gear being inspected for explosives as we were about to go into a war zone was not lost on us. When they were finished, the MPs loaded our gear onto their trucks and carted it away.

The rising sun was our cue to get moving, and we all loaded onto a bus. As we took our seats, Jake turned to me. "Pass me your cell phone," he said.

"What do you need that for?"

He was already fiddling with his own phone. "We have to turn off our service before we leave," he said. "It'd be crazy to pay for cell service in Iraq."

That was the moment it really hit me. We were leaving the country. Heck, we were leaving civilization. It felt so final, like we were giving up our last connection to the real world. *But there wouldn't be much use for a cell phone in Iraq*, I thought. *They might not even work there.*

Before we left, the governor spoke to us. We were apparently the first unit from New Mexico heading out, and he made sure to mention that fact six or seven times, as if it made us braver or more impressive somehow. He told us that if we didn't come back, he'd make sure our kids received the finest education, with as many scholarships as they needed to follow their dreams. His speech was sobering. It was odd to look around at my company and think about the possibility that some of us might not come back. And if Saddam decided to use any of those weapons of mass destruction, maybe none of us would be coming back. After a while, I started to tune the governor out. His speech was mostly a show for the media. It didn't seem to be for our benefit.

The speech ended, and we started the long, slow walk out to the tarmac. Single file the whole way, as if to heighten the drama of the moment. I wished that the plane were closer. As it was, catering to the press meant that we had to walk something like a quarter of a mile out to the plane, carrying our gear the whole way, baking in the hot Texas morning.

We boarded the plane wearing full battle rattle: Kevlar helmets, flak vest, gas mask, rifle, and all the other basic military equipment. Remember, that's more than fifty pounds of equipment, or half my body weight. And yeah, that's right, we got on the plane with our *rifles*. They rested nicely between our seats.

We were all excited, and we were all a little on edge. It was like we'd forgotten that there were still seven thousand miles between us and the war. The mood almost made the flight a pleasure—we even had real food (well, airplane food) and flight attendants. Watching the clouds drift by below, I recast the mission as an exotic honeymoon. Looking back on it now, I wasn't that far off.

We stopped at JFK and then Rome. We flew twenty hours before landing in Kuwait, and the closer we got, the more nervous I felt. Should we expect bullets to fly over our heads? Would grenades and bombs be exploding all around us? Would we need to don the gas masks right away?

The sun was just setting when we stepped off the plane, two calendar-days later, April 23, 2003. No bombs. No bullets.

Kuwait was more or less as safe as the US, but the sudden, oppressive heat was an underestimated danger. As if we'd unknowingly stepped into an oven. Within seconds, I was drenched in sweat. And then, a few seconds after that, I was dry again. The environment sucked the moisture from our uniforms, leaving a noticeable layer of salt on our clothing and skin. I could feel how hot and heavy the air was, just by breathing it in. Even a faint breeze felt like a hair dryer pointed at me. I've never been great with heat—my summers in Iowa were usually punctuated with complaints about the temperature—but I'd always been able to cope before; I just hoped I could do it here too.

We unloaded the airplane ourselves. Even the simplest task took twice as long in the heat. We all wanted to avoid going into the cargo hold (the temperature of which made the heat outside seem bearable) and had to resort to taking turns. I couldn't believe how quickly the energy was sapped from us. My body had never craved water like that. Tasks that had been matter-of-fact and easy back in Texas now felt grueling. Twenty hours on a plane and then straight to work. We were wrung out. But that's what being in the army is: beating back fatigue and fear and then giving them the finger.

A sergeant showed us to our tent. Camp Safir had hundreds of twenty- by fifty-foot canvas tents, but only one for our whole company. I thought it was a joke when we were shown one tent and told, "Get settled in." Maybe they meant just our platoon? No such luck. As we found a spot on the dirty plywood floor (no cots, no beds, just floor space), Jake and I made sure to get spots next to each other. There was just enough room for all of us to lie down, but not much more. Shoulder to shoulder, in four rows of sleeping bags on the floor. Welcome to Kuwait.

Jake and I didn't mind sharing a tiny space on the plywood, but when it came to the company's collective BO, everybody had limits.

Even though the accommodations were less than ideal, Jake and I still found time for each other—by which I mean that on occasion, we flagrantly disregarded the delicate sensibilities of our fellow soldiers and, under cover of darkness, got pleasantly busy. We did try to hold off until everyone else was asleep, but no system is perfect. We were once caught by SPC Bazzie—who shouted out in the middle of the night, "Hey, Rads! I can hear you, and I know what you're doing." SPC Bazzie was my polar opposite: Naturally social, loud, and wildly flirtatious. She was kind of rough around the edges—she really enjoyed making people uncomfortable—but was always good for a laugh.

Before joining up, that sort of thing would have mortified me. But army life strips all that anxiety and social pressure away. These people were already becoming something more than friends, closer to family. There is a level of familiarity that you have with fellow soldiers, due to the circumstances you are thrust into, that you might not have with even close family and friends.

We were in Camp Safir as a sort of buffer zone—a place where we could adjust to the area in relative safety. In this part of the world, many things want to kill you. Scorpions, snakes, sand fleas, unexploded bombs . . . the list goes on. Acclimating to the dangers was just as important as acclimating to the extremes of the environment. Not that there's any way to hurry that process along. The time difference screwed with us early on, and we never really got used to the heat.

A few days in, Skinny and I had heard that there was a tent nearby with gym equipment in it. We were still incredibly jet-lagged, so we were up at midnight—and I do mean *up*—so the rumor got our attention. Sitting around in the heat all day was causing me to lose muscle mass, and the gym sounded like just the thing. So, I dug out my gym clothes—short shorts and a cropped T-shirt—and crawled into my sleeping bag to change. I'd worn this outfit hundreds of times before, and it had never been a problem. But that was in the civilian world. We were in a new place with new rules, and I wasn't thinking about that at all. Annoyingly, Jake was. His eyes went wide as I emerged from the sleeping bag, and he took in my proposed outfit. "You can't go out like that," he said. "No way in hell."

"Why not?" I said, a little incredulous. I'd worn this outfit all the time back in Fort Bliss. What could be wrong with it?

"Seriously, Heidi. You're not in uniform. You're going to drive every male soldier on base completely nuts."

"It'll be fine," I said, draping my towel over my shoulder. "What's the worst that can happen? Will they send me into a war zone?"

Skinny and I headed for the workout tent. We didn't get more than a hundred feet before a Master Sergeant (the most feared rank in the army) passed us, did one of those cartoon double-takes, and rounded on me. "What the fuck do you think you're doing, soldier?"

My first thought was, *Aw, shit. Jake was right.* My second thought was, *He's probably right behind me, snickering.* He was.

He'd followed along to watch the show, hoping to keep me out of trouble.

The MSGT marched me back into the tent and handed me over to Top, our First Sergeant, and our unit's highest-ranking NCO—a shorter Hispanic guy with a funny mustache that made him look serious and comical all at the same time. He was all business and knew how to take care of his troops, so when he saw the MSGT marching over to him, his face fell.

"You better make damn sure this soldier never leaves the tent looking like this again," the MSGT said, his face going purple. "She's going to cause a whole bunch of trouble."

Top chewed me out pretty good for that, and I promised to retire my gym outfit for the duration of our stay. The worst part of the whole situation was Jake's face, which screamed "I told you so," even if he never actually said it.

Disagreeing with your partner is inevitable: you're both individuals with different sets of experiences. But that's why you should make a point of listening whenever the two of you think differently. The more experiences you can draw on, the wiser you'll be together.

We got word that we were moving a few days later. We were starting to adjust to the time difference, but the heat was a different story. Our gear was loaded up into a five-ton to make the trip to Camp Arifjan, but our transport was separate. And unusual. As we waited by the front gate, a bus pulled up and I instantly flashed back to the bus scene in "Romancing the Stone." The bus looked ancient, like it had been pulled out of a junkyard. Someone had spray-painted it with a Middle Eastern pattern, presumably to help us blend in with the population. I half expected to find chickens running around as I stepped onboard, but the interior was bedazzled with beads and fringe, and covered in dust, and the windows were coated in some sort of sticky residue.

We rolled out of Camp Safir, and I quickly became aware that this bus also lacked air conditioning. The heat from the climate was one thing; being stuck in a rolling tin can with your entire platoon was something different. It was sweltering. Sweat was pouring down my face, and I asked myself, *Why do people live here?* It seemed like a miserable place to exist. But then I glanced out the window and noticed that the road was filled with a Who's-Who of carmakers: Porsches, Ferraris . . . even the poor people drove Land Cruisers. Kuwait is perched on top of a lake of oil money, and that's why people live here.

The trip was short. We pulled into Arifjan and saw that things were looking up for us. This looked more like a real base, one that I might see back home. Admittedly, the "barracks" were really just airplane hangars filled with bunk beds, but all the same. It was a step up from the plywood floor in Safir. Or so we thought. The tent in Safir had at least had some air conditioning. The hangar was nowhere near that luxurious. It was boiling.

That said, Arifjan did have a few advantages over Safir. It had a PX and a real chow hall, so that first night, we simply wandered over to the chow hall, grabbed some food and sat down at one of the hundreds of folding tables in the makeshift space. I was so hungry that I couldn't wait for anyone else.

When Skinny sat down, he was his usual unreadable self, until he picked up a copy of *Stars and Stripes*, a military newspaper.

"Hey, look at this," he said pointing to the front-page article.

I read the headline. "Mission Accomplished?" I said, confusion creeping into my voice. "If the mission is accomplished, then what are we doing here?" The photo accompanying the article showed President Bush standing in front of a big banner, the words "Mission Accomplished" blazing across a field of stars and stripes.

"Maybe this is as close as we'll get," Skinny suggested. "We might stay here a few months and go home."

Sitting around Camp Arifjan being cooked in the hangars all summer sounded miserable, but nonetheless, a rumor spread through the platoon that we were going to go back as fast as we came and that we'd missed it. That we'd missed the whole war. I was pretty upset. All this time, all this effort, and now what?

I needn't have been upset. A few days later, Jake and I were walking through the PX to find something to do, and I came across a rack of T-shirts. They were on clearance, and they had "Mission Accomplished" printed across the front in big white letters. In hindsight, it's easy to see why they'd be getting rid of them so quickly.

The hours crawled by more slowly every day. We spent a lot of our time playing Risk and doing equipment maintenance, generally losing our minds with the boredom and the waiting.

It's easy to underestimate the profound and destructive effects of boredom. We had all signed up for a life of action

127

and excitement—rappelling off mountainsides and staving off the enemy as bullets whizzed past overhead, etc. We were all the sort of people who gravitate toward adventure and risk. And there was nothing like that here . . . with one possible exception: this place had cobras.

There are a lot of historical reasons for not leaving a bunch of soldiers to their own devices. Page through any book of military history and you'll come across story after story of crazy shit that went down just because a company of soldiers was stuck someplace with nothing to do for too long and eventually went stir crazy. It's a basic hazard of military life—one that officers work pretty hard to circumvent, usually with middling success. The classic tactic is weighing soldiers down with transparently make-work tasks. One such job was what we called "the police line."

During the police line, we (by which I mean the whole unit) would be sent out to an open field. We'd form a long line, making sure around five feet separated each of us. We'd turn toward the field—just the scrub and the sand between us and the horizon—and we'd walk forward. We each had a five-foot square of responsibility, and as we moved through the desert, our job was to look for trash within that five-foot square. You know how you sometimes see cop shows on TV and the police are combing the terrain for clues? That was us, but for garbage.

I wasn't impressed with this exercise. I'm sure it wasn't completely pointless—maybe someone needed to clear the area for the sake of erecting a new building or digging a new septic line or something—but it was never clear that this task was valuable in any way. Sure, it made the field on the outskirts of camp slightly tidier, but at the end of the day, it was still empty desert.

It didn't take me long to get fed up with the whole job, but it wasn't like I could just bolt and spend the time doing something fun; there was nothing fun to do. And that was when I remembered the cobras. We'd had a briefing on them early in the day—apparently someone had spotted one on the way back from the bathroom—and we'd been warned that there could be cobras in the very field we were policing. They wanted us to be careful—to shout out if we came across one and under no circumstances try to touch it. But I had no interest in just "coming across one." That was too reliant on luck and happenstance. No, I wanted to find one. I wanted to go on a cobra hunt.

So, as my unit plodded forward, slow, searching, step after step, I picked up a stick and started poking it into every hole in the ground that I came across. The cobra had to be hiding in one of these holes, I knew it. And I was going see it for myself.

I just told you that bored soldiers get up to some crazy mischief. Well, this cobra hunt was probably the most stir crazy I ever got. I was zonked enough to think that finding a poisonous snake in the wild was somehow going to turn into a cute story about silly-old Heidi, trying to befriend another citizen of the animal kingdom. Like I said, boredom makes you crazy. Luckily, I had Jake to pull me back. He saw what I was doing, stepped out of line, and came up to me. "You're smarter than this," he said. "The last thing we need is for you to get bitten by a damn cobra."

He wasn't wrong. And the sting of the Gym Clothes Incident was still fresh in my mind. I put down my stick, and we went back to collecting trash. No less bored, but a little more prudent, at least.

The days went on like that: mindless tasks and dull downtime. And then, just when we'd begun to think that this was our permanent station and we were destined to sit out whatever was left of the war, we got the word. The time we spent in Arifjan felt like months, but it was only days.

"Listen up," called our captain, as we gathered round one evening. "We just got our orders to head into Iraq. We leave tomorrow morning at 0600 hours."

CHAPTER 11

On the Road

Our convoy rolled out bright and early. Koster was behind the wheel, humming a tune I couldn't quite place. It was too early. I couldn't manage the same cheeriness. He saw me looking at him. "You know what I'm looking forward to?" he asked.

"What?"

"Beer," he said, to all appearances serious.

"When you get home, you mean?"

"No, when we get to Baghdad."

I laughed. "Baghdad's full of Muslims, dude. You'd have a better shot of finding beer on the moon."

"See, you're wrong there," he said. "You're forgetting the principle of prohibitory requirement."

"The princi-whatwhatwhat?"

"You know—the thing that makes forbidden stuff sexy."

I couldn't tell if he was making this stuff up. "You're telling me that beer is sexy?" I had a brief vision of Koster holding a dripping wet beer, still cold from the ice chest, and kissing it gently.

"I'm saying that by forbidding Muslims from drinking alcohol, they ensured that somewhere in Baghdad, probably on a busy street corner, there'll be a guy with a falafel cart selling beer under the table, and I'll be *all* over it."

I couldn't help it. I giggled. He grinned.

"You gotta learn how to lighten up, Radkiewicz," he said. "Could be anything up ahead."

Sergeant Koster, the comedian of the unit. He had been a mailman back in civilian life, but I couldn't imagine a post office that matched him. He had overly exaggerated reactions to whatever crazy situation we got ourselves into, and it was incredibly easy to make him laugh. His easygoing sense of humor meshed well with mine. We were alike in many ways, but he took easygoing to the next level.

I laughed and flipped him off. "I'm plenty light," I said, "and whatever's ahead, I can handle."

At that moment, it felt true. Trundling down the road as the sun slowly rose on the horizon, my rifle leaning up against the dash, my Kevlar a reassuring weight. And as the morning grew brighter, our visibility grew clearer—though there wasn't a whole lot to see. Sand, mostly. A few camels and their herders. And it was fine. I was fine.

But we kept getting closer to the border.

We were heading into Iraq, an actual war zone, and no one knew what to expect. There was a very solid chance that something bad could happen to us. Riding shotgun as Koster kept the semi moving with the convoy, with nothing to do but sit and watch and ruminate, I kept thinking about bombs exploding and bullets whizzing past. I kept hearing the hiss of an open gas canister.

With every turn in the road, I felt my heart speed up. There was something—it felt like an angry possum, I swear—scrambling around inside my guts, trying to get out. I tried the usual breathing techniques, but—shit, this was a real war zone—my fight or flight response kicked in. Deep-breathing techniques went right out the window.

Trying to keep my cool, I looked over at Koster. "Border's coming up," I said. "Think we'll be attacked?"

His expression didn't change. Totally unflappable. "Your guess is as good as mine, but we're in freaking semi-trucks and carrying automatic weapons. I wouldn't worry about it too much."

This was not as helpful as I'd hoped it would be.

I don't know if this happens to you, but when I get really anxious, I get gut problems. Koster telling me not to worry got my insides roiling even faster.

We rolled through the border. I spent those five minutes unabashedly scanning our surroundings, looking for any sign of the enemy. My weapon no longer resting on the dash, but aimed cautiously out the window, a practice I would soon be more comfortable with.

I saw the Iraq equivalent of Juarez, a slummy border town that made it very clear that I was in a third world country at war. It looked filthy and violent. We saw kids running around, dirty and hungry-looking. We saw women working in the dirt of the fields, and we saw men sitting around and smoking. There were people all over this little town. There was no way to tell which ones were just bystanders, and which ones might want to kill us.

But no one made a move toward us, and nothing exploded, so we kept moving. Still, my guts were not soothed. As we made it to the other edge of town and started down the highway, it got to the point where I knew we'd have a problem. I looked over at Koster. "I need a bathroom," I said, trying to keep the panic out of my voice.

Koster didn't understand. "We're in a convoy, Radkiewicz. We're not pulling over. I don't think there's a rest stop for another seven thousand miles."

A hundred semi-trucks barreling down the Iraqi road, one right after the other. No shit we're not pulling over. "I know," I said, in my strongest do-not-mess-with-me tone. "And I'm telling you, I can't wait. Not even a couple minutes."

He glanced over at me, saw my expression. And he laughed a little. "Girl," he said, "you do what you've got to do. My eyes are on the road."

After a minute of frantic searching, I found an empty MRE bag. It would have to do. I propped my flak vest between me and the console so Koster couldn't watch (not that he wanted to, but just in case), and I stripped off my boots, pants, and underwear. With the MRE bag beneath me (and my pants hanging out the window, flapping against the side of the truck), I squatted down between my seat and the dashboard.

"Sing me something, Sergeant!" I shouted, desperate for enough noise to drown out the inevitable. He giggled and started singing "Sweet Home Alabama" at the top of his lungs. I couldn't believe this was happening. I was taking a crap inside a semi-truck while barreling down the road, going through Iraq. How many people can say the same?

Eventually, the stench hit Koster. "Oh, man, that's just nasty! Toss that shit out the window!"

I was relieved to do so, though I also felt a bit bad. What if someone found it? I was sure the truck behind us had seen—at the very least—my pants hanging out the window. They had to be wondering what the hell was going on with us. I was hoping that Jake wouldn't notice my pants hanging out the window; I can't imagine what he would have thought.

When the convoy eventually pulled over—not for me, a truck had blown a tire up the line—Koster handed me his toiletry bag and said, "Here, douse that shit with my cologne."

I spent all the time we had on the side of the road scrubbing out that bit of floor. I even got the brushes out to clean up the grooves in the floor mat. I'd say I was embarrassed, but the truth is that when things get bad enough, you lose all modesty. At this point, the only thing I cared about was making the cab livable for the rest of the journey.

We made it out onto a road called Highway One—or Highway of Death, if you want to be dramatic—which would look like a normal four-lane highway if it weren't for the burnt-out vehicles that lined the sides of the road. The destruction lasted for miles. There weren't any bodies; just mile after mile of exploded Iraqi military vehicles dating back to the 1990s and Operation Desert Storm. Why didn't they clean up this stretch of highway? *Who knows? It's Iraq.*

We eventually reached Camp Tallil, about five miles outside Nasiriyah. We didn't bother getting all the way into base.

Our convoy pulled over and lined up on the side of the road, just inside the entrance to the camp. We weren't staying here long-term, because this wasn't really a stop. It had used to be a base, that was clear—rubble and pieces of blown-up concrete were everywhere. The ground was covered in a fine powdery dust that got on and in everything.

But regardless of the site being a blown-to-smithereens Iraqi air base, this was where we were spending the night. We set up camp, and I reunited with Jake. I'd never been so glad to see him. I just about knocked him to the ground.

"Babe," he said, as my grip around him lessened, "I was two trucks up. We've been—at max—a hundred meters apart from each other."

Obviously, I'd missed him—even if he had been physically close, it wasn't like we could pick up a radio and just chat—but it was more than that. We were supposed to share everything with each other, anxieties and embarrassments and all. "I dunno," I said. "I just got really nervous as we were crossing the border—"

"Aww," he said, drawing me closer.

"—and my guts went crazy and—" He drew a little away from me here. "I kind of took a shit in an empty MRE bag and then threw it out the window."

Jake took a second to gape at me, and then he laughed and pulled me back in. "Of course. We spend one day in separate trucks and you come back with a poop story." I just about melted into his arms. All my anxieties—all of those war-zone preconceptions—lessened as soon as I knew I had Jake back with me. "You know," Jake was saying, "You . . .

and your family . . . are just obsessed with bodily functions. It's kind of gross."

That night, we set up our cot on top of his trailer and watched the stars shift over the ruins of the base. I was happy and relieved to have my husband sleeping by my side.

The next day, our convoy pushed on, this time on a road called Tampa. Not much more than a worn washboard path in the desert and riddled with huge potholes, Tampa was the literal definition of hell on our wheels. Every truck threw up a plume of dust into the windshield of the truck behind it. There were times when the dust was so bad that you couldn't see the tail end of the truck ahead of you. Being in a semi was no comfort. Even though we had some solid American-made steel between us and the truck ahead of us, that truck might slam to a stop without any warning. Every turn of our tires was a danger.

As the convoy inched along, we started seeing road signs for Baghdad, and the closer we got, the greener the scenery became. Baghdad sits between the two great rivers of the area: the Tigris and the Euphrates, which were the agricultural foundation of ancient Mesopotamia. The shift from a land-scape marked by dirt and sand into one historically known as the Fertile Crescent was unexpected and a welcome change from the desert.

Amusingly, the road signs were in both Arabic and English, as if Saddam was expecting us and didn't want us to get lost. How thoughtful.

Our final stop was a small camp outside of Baghdad. A couple other companies had also set up camp here, though we never learned what they were there for. The camp was nothing more than an old factory and a meeting place for trucks. A hastily constructed barrier marked the perimeter. No water, no latrines, no nothing. We were so glad when we were told we'd be moving on in the morning. No one wanted to stay here longer than we had to.

That night, Jake and I set up a private water-bottle shower for ourselves by stringing ponchos around the catwalk of Jake's truck. There was a grate to keep our feet out of the mud, and the catwalk—the space between the cab and the trailer—was just big enough for the both of us. In that moment, the sun-warmed water streaming over our tired, dirty bodies felt just as good as the jacuzzi jets in a five-star hotel.

The shower was lit only by the stars, bright overhead, and there was a sort of gentle silence in the countryside (if you could tune out that distant *rat-tat-tat*). The sort of quiet that comes from being surrounded by acres and acres of nobody. When we'd moved to Albuquerque, I'd forgotten how gentle and safe that silence felt, but here, in this shower, if I closed my eyes and pretended, I could almost feel like I was back on my mom and stepdad's farm. And now I had Jake with me. It was a moment of private, intimate companionship. Both of us trying to make the most of our time together—skin slipping past skin, the stickiness of the blazing heat outside softening under the stream of water. I felt Jake's hands on my hips. He bent to kiss me as I turned to put my arms around him.

That was when the flash went off.

It was bright—clearly inside the shower and not just somewhere in the camp—and it came from above, over the poncho-curtain. Jake immediately understood what it meant:

some asshole was taking pictures of us. "Stay here," he said, gruffly, and scrambling into a pair of shorts, launched himself off the back of the catwalk. I pulled one of the shower curtains/ ponchos close, covering myself in case someone came past, and stepped to the edge of the catwalk. Jake had flown off the catwalk, moving at speeds I'd never seen from him before. The pervert, SPC Johnson, was on the ground in front of him, bruises already blossoming on his face. Without a word, Jake—clad only in army PT shorts and boots, but righteous in his fury—tore the camera out of Johnson's hands.

"Hey, come on," Johnson said, slowly getting to his feet. "It was just a joke."

Jake just stood there, steely-eyed, staring Johnson down.

"Apologize," Jake said. I could practically hear him counting to ten in his head. I knew it was a lost cause. Johnson wasn't the sort of guy to be ashamed of a "prank."

"Come on, man. You guys already get to be with each other—I just have myself. How's that fair?"

I watched as Jake apparently reached the end of his count. He looked one more time at Johnson, giving him one last chance, and then he took two steps away, towards a little cluster of rocks on the ground.

Johnson could see where this was headed. "Hey, man, come on," he pleaded, but Jake was undeterred. Without waiting a minute longer, he dropped the camera on the rocks and stomped it to pieces with his boot. Even from the catwalk, I could hear the crunch of glass and plastic.

"That—that cost me like three hundred dollars," said Johnson, stunned.

"Pity you didn't take care of it, then," Jake said, and headed back to me.

Jake climbed up into the shower with me. The bottle above had run dry, so he got to work fixing it while I watched Johnson for a minute longer. He sat cross-legged by the rocks, collecting his crushed camera, and something about this posture reminded me of a kicked dog, his tail between his legs, aware that he'd done something wrong, but ultimately ignorant of what it was. He certainly deserved to lose his camera. But watching him made me feel sorry for him—the nearest Best Buy was seven thousand miles away, so he had no way of replacing it—but finally, I turned away, looking for the man who always had my back.

We heard gunfire in the surrounding countryside all night. We couldn't tell where it came from exactly, but our best guess suggested neighbors settling long-standing feuds, not insurgents heading toward us. It wasn't that close, and we were pretty sure that we were safe, but it was the first time I was lulled to sleep by gunfire. It wouldn't be the last.

CHAPTER 12

Anaconda

"Freaking A, Koster," I said, my face plastered to the window, "What the heck is that?" Outside, we were passing what looked like a half-finished, or maybe half blown-up (tough to tell) storage unit, garage doors and all. I could tell it was the first floor of what was supposed to be a multilevel building. Despite the dilapidation, the locals had occupied the structure and set up little shops in the bays.

"I think it's the Baghdad equivalent of a shady strip mall?"

"That's crazy. This place is all torn up!"

"Shit, Rad, what did you think we were gonna find? Macy's? A Nordstrom, maybe?"

"No, smart ass. I was hoping for a Dairy Queen and a Walmart."

I knew that Baghdad was going to be rough. The air force had spent the last month and a half bombing it. But this . . .

the devastation far exceeded my expectations. As far as I could tell, these people had never culturally advanced beyond the age of Jesus. It was hard to believe that this place had—recently, at least—been a serious city center, with commerce and some form of normal life for these people.

"War-torn" doesn't really describe it. There was a lot of rubble where homes and businesses once stood. Many of the buildings still standing had giant holes blown in them. But it was more than that. It felt a lot like society in general had broken down. Iraqi drivers didn't seem to recognize any known traffic laws, choosing instead to dart in and out of intersections, heedless of oncoming traffic (but I'm not sure this was any different before the war). Gangs of children roamed the streets, while the stench of garbage and human waste filled the air.

Seeing the destruction drove home the reality of the war in a way that nothing else had. It made me think about how precious life is, and how lucky I was to live in the United States.

We spent most of the day trying to keep civilian drivers from getting between our trucks. Any car that comes between the trucks of a convoy—anything that attempts to isolate one part of the unit from another, in other words—could be the beginning of an ambush or suicide bomber. We had a lot of leeway for driving aggressively. Did we need to nose a car off the road? No problem. Get it done. Did we have to run someone over? Fine, do that too. Whatever it took to keep a guy with a bomb out of our convoy.

The rules of the road in Iraq are: there are no rules. Our convoys were constantly coming up against people, animals, and other vehicles, and in that kind of contest, the convoy always wins. That said, nobody wants to run over a civilian, or their livestock, so we try to be aware of how people are moving around us, whether they're walking, riding their bikes, driving their cars, or herding their animals. They didn't seem to care that a mile-long line of eighteen-wheelers was plowing through the town, so we had to be a little aggressive with them from time to time.

You spend your whole life living in a place where breaking the law has consequences. So, when you're suddenly dropped into a place where your life depends on breaking some of those laws, your mind hesitates. The army did a really good job of training that hesitation out of us when it came to shooting at the enemy, but we never learned how to deal with infiltration into our convoy. Every time I got into my semi, I found myself second-guessing my decisions. Should I push that car out of the way? Should I shoot at them? Should I let them go through? It was never clear. You never knew who was the enemy or who was just a moron, testing the patience of a trigger-happy soldier. It was purely a guessing game. I decided to err on the side of staying alive, and luckily the locals understood the universal language of being threatened with an M16.

Our destination, Camp Anaconda, was about an hour north of Baghdad. We parked our trucks and trailers, and set up for the night. There was no word on what was next, so Jake and I reused the previous night's plan: we set up our cots on top of the trailer, draped everything in mosquito netting to fend off the bugs, and turned in. Jake wrapped his arms around me as mortars crashed nearby, and tracers sped through the distant sky. For the first time, we were close to the fight. So close that you could hear the *thunk* of the mortars as they were launched at us.

In the morning, there were no new orders. Just the oppressive heat, and an aimlessness that gripped even our captain. Everyone spent the day sitting around, waiting for something to do. A few of us got crafty and sat by the road with handmade signs: "Will work for food or beer." No takers.

The next day we got word that this was where we were setting up camp. We couldn't know how long we'd be there. We put up some tents—temporary barracks divided by gender (we had it easy back then, there were only two genders and it was obvious which one you were). That meant Jake and I weren't bunking together anymore. After setting up camp, we still didn't have much to do. The heat was crushing. It weighed on us like a lead blanket. Dealing with boredom on any base is a serious skill, and this wasn't even much of a base yet. You've only got what you've brought with you, so you've got to make the best of it. We played catch, and we made signs to decorate the tents—at one point, the guys made an elaborate tent entrance out of wood and palm fronds—and we wandered around the camp looking for trouble. In a previous life, Anaconda had been an Iraqi air base, so we spent a fair amount of time poking around shelled-out buildings, pretending to be archaeologists studying an ancient ruin. It's funny, the things you'll do when heat and boredom are slowly driving you crazy.

We spent a week that way. The thrill of a new place wears off pretty quickly, and soon enough your day-to-day chores become the things that define your life. You never think about laundry until you don't have access to a washing machine. What with the heat and the sand, it took no time at all for our uniforms to get crusty, and the only way to get them clean was to hand wash them.

We had a couple of little, pink tubs—one for washing and one for rinsing—and we'd set up a tiny laundry station on the only piece of concrete around to avoid making mud. "I bet you never thought you'd be hand-washing clothes in Baghdad on your honeymoon," Jake said, smirking at me.

"Yeah. It's kind of like *Little House on the Prairie*," I said, pulling a pair of Desert Camouflage Uniform (DCU) pants from the murky water. "I never thought I would be washing anything by hand, much less in Baghdad."

Jake grinned. "Someday, we'll go on a real honeymoon, and if you're lucky, I won't even make you wash our clothes by hand."

I splashed some of the disgusting brown wash water at him, and got him when he wasn't looking. "You'd better believe we're going on a honeymoon after this. And there'll be no laundry at all. Period."

Jake pulled an undershirt out of the rinsing water and hung it on a line. When he came back, his face was serious. "You know," he said, "this isn't the traditional way people spend their honeymoon, but you've got to admit, it's kind of cool being here together. How many husbands and wives get to experience something like this? I mean, after this, what could life possibly throw at us that we can't handle?"

I thought about that for a minute. We had been so wrapped up in making sure we were here together, that I'd never really considered the uniqueness of our situation. Here we were: newly married, deployed in a war zone, and in the same platoon. Women in combat were a fairly new concept, but I had never heard of a married couple in combat before. It really made me remember that God was looking out for us.

"How about kids?" I said, and grinned, breaking the mood.

Jake laughed. "Don't even go there."

"Yeah, better wait until after the real honeymoon."

"Seriously, though. As strange as it sounds, we are really lucky to be here together."

* * *

After a week of nothing, we got our first proper mission. The briefing was short: Convoy down to Saddam's palace in Baghdad and deliver supplies. At this point in the war, there wasn't much going on. The Iraqi Republican Guard had been decimated, and there hadn't been any big insurgent uprisings . . . yet. We had no idea that the route we would take to the airport the next day would eventually come to be called "I.E.D. Alley"—one of the most dangerous roads in Iraq.

"No big deal," Koster said, as we climbed into the semi. "Just rolling through Baghdad to the palace of an ex-dictator. Just a little jaunt into the most populated area of Baghdad. Practically a day trip to the beach. Bring enough toilet paper, Rad?"

"Bite me, Koster," I said, and pulled the door shut.

When we arrived in Baghdad, I had this strange moment where I was sure that if you squinted, you could see the old parts of the city, the Baghdad before the war, the city that— regardless of how corrupt its government had been—had at least managed to sustain some semblance of normalcy. I thought there must be some remnants of that city underneath all the carnage and destruction we passed through on our way to the palace. That idea lasted about as long as it took to pull the trucks through the palace gates.

Back home, I'd never expected to see this place. You know how there are some landmarks that you figure you'll see someday? Places like the Glacier National Park or Yosemite, or the White House, even. Well, Saddam's Palace was nowhere on that list for me, but as we got closer, I found myself getting more and more intrigued. We had heard stories from other soldiers on base, but more importantly, it was something new, something to relieve the boredom. From this place, Saddam Hussein had terrorized his people. He'd lived parts of his day-to-day life here, as well as in palaces like this one strewn about the country. The fact that we were about to occupy the same buildings and grounds that this monster had inhabited gave me an uneasy feeling.

We approached the gates—our whole convoy, one long line—and I stuck my head out the window for a better look. From a distance, it didn't look all that impressive. Just a big concrete wall that was at least ten to fifteen feet tall. But then I noticed something strange. See, in everyplace I've lived—Eagle Grove, Fort Collins, Albuquerque—it's easy to see where the money is. There's always a fancy neighborhood, and at the center of that neighborhood is the fanciest house. The biggest, prettiest, most pleasantly landscaped private building in the city. Saddam's palace was clearly going to be that place. But unlike those other neighborhoods, where the best house is surrounded by not-quite-as-nice-but-still-quite-nice houses, Saddam's palace was surrounded by dilapidated homes, shacks, and garbage. Back-bending poverty. The disparity was deeply weird.

Inside the walls, things were just as opulent as I had imagined. Acres of exquisitely engineered streams and turquoise pools, some of them dotted with their own manufactured islands and intricately crafted minipalaces, all surrounded by lush greenery and huge palm trees. It was beautiful. And I couldn't help reflecting that, considering how dry the rest of the country was, a palace surrounded by water seemed incredibly cruel.

Our convoy made its way down the long road to the center of the compound: the palace itself. The water, although dirty, was inviting—I wasn't at all surprised to see off-duty soldiers fishing in it. If we hadn't been convoying, if it had been just Jake and me, we would have stopped right there, in the middle of the road, and tried our luck too. But we had jobs to do.

We pulled the semis into the parking lot around the back and hopped out. The unit stationed at the palace sauntered out to help us unload. Afterwards, I found Jake in the shade. "We've got an hour before we head out," he said, as I approached. "What do you want to see first?"

"We could go fishing," I said.

"I thought you wanted to see the palace," he said. "Don't you want to see what's inside?"

I did want to see the palace. But I also wanted to kick back and do something normal, something that I'd always enjoyed back at home.

Jake saw me wavering. "Someone said there was air conditioning . . ."

That did it. I was off like a shot, dragging Jake behind me, and before we knew it we were wandering around this ridiculously ornate building that had been turned into a PX. We blissfully luxuriated in the industrial-strength air conditioning, our footsteps tapping across mosaic floors, our voices echoing through rooms covered in floor-to-ceiling tile work. We weren't allowed into the main palace—that was reserved for the top brass, so this would have to do—but it was nice being inside a real building, with real glass windows, and real air conditioning. Soldiers were loitering around the makeshift PX shop just to cool off, not really interested in anything the shop sold.

The trip back to Anaconda was largely uneventful, with lots of traffic and angry people getting bumped off the road. But when we finally pulled in to camp that evening, tired and stressed, we learned that there would be no true respite from the journey. A rumor was circulating: we'd be moving out the next day. Rest was clearly something only civilians got to enjoy.

CHAPTER 13

Fallujah

The next morning, we heard the official word: we had just a few hours to pack up our entire camp and load everything back onto the trucks. It seemed like moving was getting to be a regular thing. I began to wonder if we'd somehow been signed up for the gypsy transportation company and no one had told us.

The road out took us through downtown Fallujah. I know what you're thinking—wasn't that a hotbed of insurgency? Sure, that's what it eventually became, but at the time we were there, we figured it was just another crappy town in Iraq. Not that you couldn't see the signs of what was coming. The mood on the street was more hostile than anything we had seen yet, and the collective unease made the hair on the back of your neck stand straight up.

As our convoy entered the town, it was pretty clear that we weren't welcome. We'd passed through other towns, and while it wasn't unusual for the convoy to get the occasional sullen glare, most people just went about their business. Not so in Fallujah. Here, as we entered the town center, the majority of the people outside (mostly men, who seemed to spend their time in cafes) stopped whatever they were doing to watch us pass, their faces a sea of discontent and disdain. Some of them made offensive hand gestures, or stood up to face us, or pointedly set down their cups of tea, staring at us the whole time, as if to say, "Don't mind us. It's too hot right now, but we'll try to kill you later." It wasn't a great feeling.

The kids were a different story, though. They ran after us, and crowded around our trucks whenever we stopped, smiling and holding their hands out for candy or money or . . . anything, I guess. They didn't have much and quite honestly, neither did we.

The kids were what tipped us off to something being wrong.

"That's weird," I said to Koster. "I've seen that kid before."

"Which one?"

"The one with the scrubby shirt on."

"They're all wearing scrubby shirts."

"Yeah, but that one—" I was trying not to point. I didn't know what was considered rude here. "That one, I've seen him like three times so far. Are—are we going around in circles? Or is he just a super-fast runner?"

Koster had been concentrating on keeping pace with the truck ahead of us, and maybe avoiding running anyone over. "You know what? I think you're right, I remember him too."

"I think we've just been circling the town square."

"What the freak? There must be something wrong." Koster's hand went to his rifle, an instinct telling us we were in danger. "LT Styles is leading the convoy today. Scale of one to stupid, how likely do you think it is that we're lost because of that idiot?"

"I dunno, man," I said, glancing out the window. We'd left the latest pack of kids behind, and were now—much too slowly for comfort—passing a series of outdoor cafes. The men sitting at the tables outside did not look happy to see us. Again.

"LT's gonna get us killed," Koster muttered, squinting at the windshield, trying to see the truck at the head of the line.

"Most likely," I said, my grip on my weapon tighter than I'd expected it to be.

The truck ahead of us stopped, so we stopped too. I was keeping an eye on the locals—I'd heard too many stories about innocent-looking Iraqis suddenly tossing explosives into vehicles—when I saw LT Styles picking his way down the line of trucks. He got to the one ahead of us and, trying to ignore the café customers (who, seeing a soldier unprotected by a truck, suddenly got vocal), rapped on the passenger side door. SGT Ahmed, the only Arabic-speaking soldier in our unit, poked his head out the window. I couldn't hear what they were saying, but the LT's body language was clear as day.

Ahmed got out. The LT turned to one of the café customers—one who was standing in front of the other guys and strangely, wasn't shouting. The LT said something, then turned to Ahmed, and Ahmed, with a deeply bemused expression on his face, interpreted. He used enough gestures that I could interpret without hearing anything. Koster was right.

We were lost, and Ahmed was asking directions. The LT looked pissed.

Finally, thanks to Ahmed's directions, we got loose of Fallujah, and headed south toward the unknown, toward our next camp. Compared to Fallujah, the road was a breeze. We never got up to anything approaching real speed, but we were definitely moving. The desert whizzed past.

Our final stop that trip was another camp called Camp Cedar. We pulled in as the sun went down and we lined the trucks up, one after the other, a sort of fence against the expanse of the desert. It was dark. We were dirty, hungry, and exhausted. All we wanted was to set up our cots and fall into them. But someone pulled out a bottle of booze (apparently Koster was right about finding booze here), and everyone clambered out to get some.

The day had been crazy, and no one could begrudge us an hour or so of taking the edge off. Jake and I sat on the end of our trailer; our friends arrayed around us, cracking jokes and letting the stress of the day melt away. It seemed like everyone else was doing the same, until we heard shouting.

We couldn't see much. A proper base would have had floodlights illuminating the entire area, and everything would be enclosed by berms and lookout towers, keeping everyone well within sight—but this was just a spot on the map. The line of trucks stretched into the distance, the voices coming from a spot a few trucks down. There was no way for us to see what was going on.

But we could hear just fine.

"Give me that bottle." Wilson's voice boomed out through the night air, his syllables slurring ever so slightly.

Locklear's reply was almost as loud, and just as drunk sounding. "It's mine! I'm the one who got it from the *haji*."

"I'm the one who drove all day. You just sat with your feet up on the dash."

There was a muted thud, and a crash of glass as a bottle broke.

The rest of us sat and listened, not wanting to get involved. I'm not sure what everyone else was thinking, but part of me, the bit that I try to pretend doesn't exist, wished someone else would intervene. We were so quiet that we could hear Wilson getting to his feet. "Fuck you, asshole," he said.

And then we heard a sound that all soldiers can recognize in their sleep: a round being chambered into an M-16.

That was when everything went crazy. Everyone scattered, diving for cover in the dark. Before I really understood what was happening, Jake was tugging at my arm. "Heidi, get in the truck!"

"What about the stuff?" Half our gear was just sitting on the trailer bed, ready to make camp.

"Can't use it if we're dead!" Jake yanked at my arm once more, and I shot into action.

I bolted for the cab, yanking the door open and vaulting inside. "Go!" I said, my voice husky with panic. Jake, his door hanging ajar as he tried to scramble into the seat, turned on the engine and jammed his foot down on the gas. As the truck rolled out into the desert, I listened breathlessly for gunshots, sure that they were coming.

155

Jake pulled us out to around one hundred meters away from the commotion, and we spent the rest of the night out there, taking our chances with the unknown and the dark, away from the fight and the possibility of "friendly" fire. We came back in the morning.

No one had been shot.

As far as we could tell, they'd just shouted at each other and then fallen asleep. Someone eventually got the captain involved, and he split up Locklear and Wilson, giving them different driving partners. He also put both of them on the shittiest details he could think of for the next few days as we set up camp.

I didn't spend a lot of time thinking about that night. I chalked it up to a long, stressful day, not seeing any alcohol in months, and poor judgment. But it did make me cautious about who I spent time with in our unit, and who I brought into our circle of trusted friends. It was a little scary that people who were supposed to have each other's backs were one bottle of crappy whiskey away from shooting each other. I was glad I had someone I knew I could count on.

CHAPTER 14

Camp Cedar

"Decker! Hurry up!" I shouted. The sweat was rolling off my forehead and dripping in my eyes and burning, but I couldn't let go of the pole. "Where's that damn hammer and stake?" The sun was killing me. The tent pole was holding up a couple hundred pounds of tent fabric pulling me in the other direction, and I could actually feel the sun cooking me.

"Just wipe your eyes with your shoulder." Jake said looking at me with a puzzled expression.

"You know I don't like anything dirty touching my face, my skin is sensitive!"

"What? Your face is *covered* with dirt! Do you realize how ridiculous that is?"

Jake was holding up the pole next to mine, struggling with the weight and the sun as well. This was the first tent of the day, it was barely 8:00 a.m. and I didn't know how I would get through the rest of this day. SPC Decker finally came around with the sledgehammer and pounded a three-foot-long metal stake into the ground, hard as concrete in some places. This was the perfect task for him. He was built like a football player, and you could still see the high-school athlete in him. "How you holding up, Rad?" he said, grinning. "Only another half-a-dozen tents to go."

"Shut it, Decker." I was in no mood for his jolly sledge-hammer banter. How could he function in this heat and be in such a good mood? Any day in Iraq was hotter than the hottest summer in Iowa. A glance down at my brown DCU T-shirt revealed a fuzzy white line of salt, the sweat evaporating so fast that my shirt never even felt wet.

Camp Cedar was pretty much a wasteland. Sand, diesel pumps, and a dirt berm that surrounded the more-or-less empty stretch of desert. No running water. No electricity. Just flat potential. We were literally setting up a camp from scratch.

If there had ever been a time when I thought life in Iraq would be easy—there hadn't, just go with me—setting up Camp Cedar would have blown that illusion to pieces. Out of the trucks in our convoy, we unloaded dozens of tarps, tents, stakes, latrines, showers, generators, and kitchen equipment, and then we set it all up. We'd erect tents (which, strangely, were heavy, nonbreathing, and much better suited to the mountains of Afghanistan than the Iraqi desert). We'd dig garbage pits. We'd lay cable. We'd position generators in such a way that if something went wrong with one it wouldn't light the rest of the camp on fire.

Drilling with your friends is fine—you get some idea of what they're like under pressure—but there's nothing like the real world to really test someone's mettle. And it doesn't get much more intense than hard labor in the middle of May in the Iraqi desert.

Our unit worked well as a team. Jobs would be broken up by platoon and even squad. Each company had four platoons. Each platoon had four squads. When there was a job or mission, we'd rally together and get it done.

In a lot of ways, it was there in that desert that my marital relationship with Jake was truly forged. We'd been together through what I quickly began to think of as our days of plenty—first-world comforts like paved roads and running water and giant supermarkets—but this was when we learned the truth about each other's character. If we were ever going to see each other when the going got tough, this was the moment.

When our first day in Camp Cedar came to an end, I had two things on my mind: sleep and food. I grabbed my cot and headed to the females' tent, ready to unfold its insect-like legs, and deeply glad to be done erecting things for the day. It was early evening, and while the heat didn't seem to be dissipating, the sunlight was.

"Hey, Rad," Bazzie said, setting up her cot next to mine. "Did you see the mess tent we put up on the other side of camp?"

"Mess tent? Does that mean no more MREs?"

Bazzie nodded. "I saw the cooks setting up for dinner as we finished. They had a whole kitchen trailer and everything."

Real food. Something fresh-ish, and not out of a plastic MRE bag, packed back when I was in the third grade. We had been eating nothing but MREs for weeks now, and just the thought of the cooks preparing something *real* had me salivating.

"What do you think they're cooking?" Jake asked as we navigated the maze of recently constructed tents between us and the mess.

"I don't really care as long as it's not an MRE." My stomach growled as we got close enough to start picking up the smells from the kitchen.

"You guys are in for a real treat," mumbled Skinny as we got in line.

It was always hard to tell if Skinny was being sarcastic or serious—the dude was just that deadpan—but at that moment, I wasn't patient enough to subject his tone to thorough analysis. At the head of the line, the cooks were dishing up plates, and as we got closer, I started to get a better picture of the kitchen. I saw one of the cooks open what looked like a freezer and pull out a beige tray. It was about the size of my mom's nine-by-thirteen-inch casserole pan, but plastic and sealed across the top. I watched as the cook sliced open the top of the tray and poured the contents into a big pot. There were dozens of empty trays in the garbage can next to him. There was a moment where my wishful thinking got the better of me, and I was sure that the glop in the pot was just part of the menu, and then the rose-colored glasses fell from my eyes, and I realized that these were just extra-large MREs, designed to feed a crowd. We got to the head of the line, the cook ladled glop onto my plate, and out of self-preservation, I discarded all hopes that I'd ever have decent food again. I decided to focus on looking forward to going to bed.

That night, as we made our way back to our platoon's area, totally exhausted, Jake pulled up short. "Holy crap," he said. "You see that?"

We'd come close to one of the light sets—a generator packaged with a long pole and huge lights, one of many that had been erected around the camp that morning—and there was something on it. Something moving. Jake got out his camera.

"How could you miss them?" I said. "They're as big as my hand." I knew right away what kind of bugs we were looking at. My dad had collected and mounted weird insects since his own time in college, and as a kid, I'd spent hours poring over the collection. I held my hand down next to one for scale as Jake snapped a picture. "It's a giant water bug!"

"He's got to be confused," Jake said. "There's no water here."

Confused or not, there were dozens of them—along with a bunch of other bugs—swarming each light set. I'd never seen it before, but the desert came alive at night. It was amazing.

Still enchanted by our encounter with the natural world, Jake walked me back to the females' tent. We lingered outside for a moment, holding each other in the shadows, just enjoying being close. Relishing the privacy, I reached up and kissed him goodnight, a moment of affection that we usually avoided during daylight hours.

As I fell into my cot, exhausted from the day's camp duties and still dripping with sweat (even though the sun had been down for hours), it dawned on me that our living conditions had been getting progressively worse. We'd started out with real food and running water, but now we were back to living like the pioneers. I've never been prim and proper. My fondest memories involved camping with my parents, either in a tent or the trailer. I was one of those girls who you'd find sitting on the ground, collecting bugs and analyzing Mother

Nature's beauty. But this was different. It was hard to find the beauty in Iraq. It seemed like everything wanted to kill us here: the sun, the bugs, the people. The one constant was knowing that every morning when I woke up, my husband would be by my side.

Over 120-degree days, dry, sandy, and besieged by bugs, life at Camp Cedar was a constant physical challenge. Imagine running a marathon and you'll get some idea of how hot and sweaty we were, and that was just sitting still. Getting anything done required another level of energy and resulted in another bucket of sweat.

The heat and the isolation meant that we spent most of our free time baking in the sun while writing letters home, or trying to watch a movie on a portable DVD player. Hanging out in the tents only resulted in misery—the heavy material made the interiors more like ovens than shady hideaways—so we'd put up layers of camo-netting to create patches of cover for ourselves for the sake of a partially shady area with plenty of air flow.

As we settled into our new environment, one of our new duties involved keeping the camp hydrated. The camp's entire supply of water was kept in huge, five-thousand-gallon water bladders that sat on trailers. Whenever one of them got low (which happened daily), someone had to drive it over to Camp Tallil (which had a water purification station) and fill it back up. It was the sort of thing that took the whole day, but you didn't need that many people for it. Jake and I could do it on our own without a problem: just hook up the nozzles and sit back while your five-thousand-gallon water balloon slowly inflates.

Jake and I had been waiting for the water bladder to fill when a dog wandered into our perimeter. It wasn't big, or anything, but it was scraggly, and walked with a kind of hitch to its step that made me think it needed help. It had been months since we'd consigned Cody and Barley to a life of pampering and treats with Jake's parents, and the sight of this little, potentially injured dog tugged at all of my dog-mom instincts.

As I stood up, putting out my hand to call him over, Jake sucked in a breath: "Heidi, wait—"

But I wanted to pet the dog. There was no waiting.

"Wait, Heidi—he's probably not friendly—"

Bullshit, I thought.

"He probably wants to rip our faces off—"

But I was not listening. I tutted soothingly to the pup, "Come on, baby, who's a pretty baby?"

At which point the dog's upper lip curled back in a snarl, and he went from Toto to Cujo in seconds. He may have literally been foaming at the mouth.

I yanked my hand back just in time. As Jake and I hightailed it into the cab of our truck, little Cujo snarling behind us, Jake chambered a round into his rifle, just in case. We slammed the door just as the dog tried to jump up it. "Dang," I said, my breath heaving as I tried to bring my heart rate down. "Holy crap. I did not expect that."

"No shit!" Jake said. "I didn't think he would be friendly, but I didn't expect Cujo to come out."

I flopped back in my seat, watching as the dog yelped and jumped and snarled outside our truck. "Yeah . . . I didn't believe you. I was pretty sure my heart would win him over."

Eventually, Cujo got bored waiting for us to come out and let him bite us, and he wandered off. Goes to show, though—never let your fantasies blind you to the horrors that are actually around you. Not all dogs are nice.

Driving back to camp once the bladder had been refilled was a little more challenging. Every time we accelerated, slowed down, swiveled, or turned, we could feel the bladder swaying from side to side. We spent the entire ride praying that it wouldn't come loose and burst on the road.

Back at camp, we found the platoon leaders splitting us up into groups to head over to Tallil, where, apparently, the air force had set up a PX. There were even rumors of working phones. We had been in the sandbox for a few weeks now, and most of us were starting to run out of necessities like toilet paper, soap, and toothpaste. You would think that the army would supply that kind of thing, and it does, but the guys who delivered that stuff happened to be . . . us. And we were just getting on our feet. If we wanted any of that stuff, we'd have to visit the PX. Jake and I joined a dozen or so of our platoon-mates in the back of a five-ton and rolled out.

When we arrived, we found that the PX had been set up in what looked like an Iraqi version of a school gymnasium. It looked like it had taken a beating recently. Where there should have been windows, there were only shards of broken glass. The floor was dusted with what appeared to be some sort of brown talcum powder, but underneath the dust, you could see the markings of a basketball court, or maybe decorative tile. Sunlight beamed through the broken windows, highlighting the particles of dust in the air, nearly as thick as fog. The PX's wares were laid out on folding tables, very impromptu and scattered, collecting a layer of dirt that grew thicker in the short time we were there.

"Hey, they have magazines," Jake shouted from across the room.

I sprinted over. "Ooh... Any gossip magazines?" I sorted through the array of magazines and noticed that there were a lot of *Maxim* and *Popular Mechanic* types. I was looking for *People*, but no dice. "We could just get the *Maxim* and trade off rating the chicks?"

"What? No." Jake chuckled. "I just get those for the articles."

"Sure you do, babe."

The PX's selection was pretty sparse. but it was fun to pretend that we were shopping in an actual store. The longer you've been away from home, the more compelling these little flights of fancy get. They're still just daydreams, though. Easily burst by the sight of, say, a guy with an old-school brick phone.

"Jake!" I tugged at his elbow, spinning him around. "You see that guy over there? I think he has a satellite phone! You think maybe he'll let us use it?"

"Can't hurt to try. Let's go ask him."

We walked over to the table, lingering, pretending to be absorbed in the table's contents, as the SGT finished up his conversation. We didn't want to intrude, but our subterfuge must not have been very convincing. He saw us, and held up his finger, motioning for us to wait.

"What can I do you for?" he asked.

"We were wondering if we could use your phone to call back home?"

He shrugged. "Sure. But it's not my phone, it's the air force's. And you'll have to wait your turn like the rest of us." And he pointed behind me to a long line, stretching halfway across the room.

Jake and I waited in line for about an hour for the phone, and were only allowed to use it for five minutes. I could feel my anxiety building as my turn approached. What would I say to my parents? "Hey guys, I'm still alive. I love you. Bye!" There was so much more to say.

I was so absorbed in trying to work out what I wanted to say that I almost didn't notice when the guy ahead of me finished his call. He passed the phone into my hands, gave me a very quick tutorial in dialing internationally on a satellite phone, and left me to it.

"Hello?" my mom answered.

"Hi mom, it's Heidi." There was a weird delay in her response.

"OH HONEY, are you okay? I'm so relieved to hear your voice!"

"Yes mom, I'm doing just fine. I've only got a few minutes . . ."

We talked about the conditions in Iraq and how things were going back home. She asked if we had seen any combat yet. I didn't tell her that we had been close enough to hear the combat and see the tracers. I didn't want her to worry. There's a hard moment that comes with calling home. On the one hand, you just want a little moment where everything is like it was—innocent and upbeat, unconcerned with roadside bombs or whether or not today was the day you died of heatstroke—but on the other hand, you know that things will

166

never be the same, and that you're just opening up a chasm of experience that's always going to separate you from the people you've loved your whole life.

I waited for Jake to get off the phone with his parents and when he did, we walked together back to the trucks.

Camp Cedar was a transport hub. Somewhere for transportation companies like ours to park their convoys and bunk up for a night or two. We were all working together to bring supplies north, and the camp had to be available to more companies than just ours, which meant that the logistics of the camp were under constant scrutiny. Trucks got parked around the tent area. There was a whole line of showers and latrines behind the tents, but there was no way for us to build a sewer. The absence of a sewer meant that the only way the contents of the latrines got reduced was through more-or-less constant maintenance. Jake and I drew the short straw only once, for one week.

Under the seat of a latrine was half of a fifty-five-gallon drum. That drum half contained a thick layer of JP8, a diesel fuel. The fuel stopped the stench and bugs from getting out of control, and it made maintaining the latrine possible. Poop patrol, as we called it, involved pulling the open drums out from underneath the latrines, and then lighting them on fire. You'd watch as the contents of the drum burned, emitting a stench that cannot be described—you'd have to smell it to understand—and then you'd refill the drums and push them back in.

Lighting shit on fire is not a romantic task. There's nothing about it that inspires passion, or even goodwill. You spend a lot of time thinking of your fellow human being as just one long, complicated tube—a poop machine, as it were—and resenting them for it. But Jake and I tackled latrine maintenance together with the same teamwork and commitment we used to get through every other aspect of our lives. Jake took charge of pulling the drums out (which was by far the worst part of the job) because he didn't want me to have to do the shittier detail of the shit detail. It's the little things, like this, that made me grateful I had a strapping man by my side, to act like a gentleman and take on the ugly bits, not because I couldn't do it, but because he didn't think that I should have to do it. Instead, I stood by the blazing drum and turned the contents with a stick, making sure that everything that could burn, did burn.

Latrine maintenance was pretty rare, as there were plenty of people to pull that duty. You only had to tick off Top once to be assigned to it. The only upside to this duty was that no one questioned you spending a little extra time in the shower that day.

The open-air showers were on a four-foot-square platform separated into two semiprivate stalls. The stall walls weren't proper walls—more like broad slabs of plywood anchored to the corner posts. Anyone looking could see feet moving around, and maybe the top of your head if you were tall enough. Each pair of showers had its own giant metal water tank (that needed to be filled up daily) holding maybe two hundred gallons of sun-warmed water. Because water was always limited, you couldn't just turn on the tap and let it pour over you. We were only allowed a shower once every couple of days, and the amount of water we could use was rationed by a spring-loaded pull chain. You'd give it a yank, and a valve would open for a few minutes before snapping shut again.

"Shhh," I whispered, pointing to the other side of the shower. Someone had just come in and we always tried to be as inconspicuous as we could when showering together.

"Everyone knows we're in here," Jake said, hanging up his towel on the lone towel hook we shared. "There's a whole line of people that just watched us walk in, and besides, they can see our feet."

I blushed a little at the thought, but figured if anyone had a problem with it, we would have already heard about it. Showering together meant that we both had a little extra time under the water, and from time to time we could get distracted from the true purpose of a shower.

As the days passed and we grew more accustomed to the camp, it started to feel more like home. We made improvements here and there that transformed it from a mess of military gear into something a bit more personal. A calendar here, a picture hung there, a favorite spot in the shade to set your cot . . . individual preferences made it just a little homier. When we settled in for the evening, Jake would drag his cot out of the tent to join the rest of the gang in comfort and ease. Some of us would spend our evenings reading new magazines from the PX and catching up on month-old news, while others would spend the time writing letters home. One by one, people would disappear into their tents for the night, and Jake and I would be left alone, neither of us wanting to separate, but both nearing exhaustion.

One evening, we found we simply couldn't stand the idea of spending the night apart. Jake was the first to suggest it. "How about you grab your cot? I'll set up some mosquito netting and we can just sleep here for the night."

"Think anyone will care?" I hoped he would say no.

"We can try. Maybe if we keep it on the down-low, no one will care."

Jake and I set up our cots, blending in with some of the camo netting draped off the side of the tent. It was almost like we had our own little honeymoon suite. As we lay there, holding each other, I heard footsteps approaching. My first thought was that we had been busted, and I braced for the inevitable chewing out.

"Hey, is Rad in there?" SSGT Macheco's voice was cautious.

"Yeah, which one?" I asked, and heard him take several steps back when he realized what might have been happening.

"I don't mean to bother you guys, but Top just told me we got a mission tomorrow, so be up at 4:00 a.m." And with that, he walked away.

We were newlyweds, together on an adventure, and no matter how hot it got, or how terrible latrine duty was, or how delicious the sand fleas found Jake's flesh, we always had each other. We leaned into each other, and that was how we survived when the shit really hit the fan.

CHAPTER 15

Pony Express

When the alarm went off, I jolted out of my cot, and my rifle fell to the ground. *Shit*, I thought. *I hope it's not caked with sand.* Jake was already putting on his boots. 4:00 a.m. I couldn't remember waking up this early, even for basic. "Did you get any sleep last night?"

"No. How could I?" Jake said, scratching at his arm. "The damn sand fleas were biting me all night long."

"Really? I didn't get any bites. I guess you're sweeter than me."

Even at 4:00 a.m. the temperature was in the upper nineties. Sweat was already beading up along my forehead.

I grabbed my sleeping bag and tiny travel pillow and shoved them inside a stuff sack, which I used as my luggage for these missions. Jake and I sneaked a quick kiss before we parted ways. "Be careful out there today. See you at Anaconda."

It was early June, and while we had just heard that major combat operations were declared completed, it didn't seem like the *haji* had gotten the memo. Every morning before a mission, in those fleeting moments before we parted ways, I felt a pit in my stomach. There was always the possibility that we wouldn't see each other again. That this kiss would be our last. We hadn't seen any combat yet, but I knew that every mission had potential dangers. But there was nothing for it. I slung my rifle on my shoulder, and Jake went the other way.

I made my way to my "official" tent. I still needed to grab a change of uniform and some things for the road. I walked in to find SPC Bazzie, still sleeping.

"Hey! Get up! We have to be in the motor pool in fifteen minutes." It wasn't like I could turn on the lights to wake her. We didn't have any lights in the tent. I fumbled around in my footlocker, trying to find my flashlight. When I found it, I shined it in her eyes.

"What the hell, Rad?" she said, slowly waking, rubbing at her face.

"Come on, get up. We've got just a few minutes." I finished packing, put on my web gear and Kevlar, and headed to the motor pool, leaving Bazzie to sort herself out.

I thought I was driving with SGT Koster, but when I got to my truck, I found SSGT T. "Hey, where's Koster?" I asked, loading my minimal luggage into the box on the back of the truck.

"We had to switch things up. They had to ship SPC Ruiz back to the States. He got some kind of infection from the sand flea bites. So Koster's riding with someone else."

"Yikes, sand flea bites?" I thought of Jake's arms, covered in bites. But I didn't have time to ruminate on it—I could hear the trucks starting up all around us, getting ready to roll out.

A Humvee drove past and stopped just in front of my truck. Supplies for the road. I grabbed a case of water out of the back, T pulled out a case of MREs, and we bungeed them down on the back of the cab. I crawled up into the truck, setting my rifle against the dash. SSGT T started the engine and waited for the air pressure to build so we could release the brakes and head out. A long line of semi-trucks stood in the dark, headlights shining out into the desert. You could smell the diesel exhaust. Dust danced in the beams of the headlights. One by one, we pulled out, forming the long convoy. We left the safety of the camp as the sun rose over the desert, and headed toward Route Tampa.

It sounds peaceful. The reality was anything but. Have you ever driven in rain so heavy that you can't tell if you're moving forward, or how fast you're going? That's what driving on Tampa was like.

"Slow down," I said, "You can't see anything, I don't even know if we're on the right side of the road!"

Sergeant T looked over at me with a smile, not even looking at the road.

"Calm down. We will be fine. I think I can still see the tail lights up ahead."

"You're not even looking. How can you see any taillights?"

The dust was impenetrable. We could barely see the truck nose through the windshield, much less anything in front of that. It wasn't unusual to drive with very limited visibility, but right now we had zero. T and I bickered, my heart racing as every foot of road passed beneath us. That was when it happened. BAM . . . a head-on collision. The truck came out of nowhere and before we knew it we had smashed into a five-ton truck in another convoy headed the opposite way. My head whipped forward, carried by the weight of my helmet. I slid down my seat, bracing myself with my arms against the dash.

"Dang it, I told you we were on the wrong side of the road!" Looking around the cab, I saw that it felt worse than it actually was. We must not have been going that fast, and the other convoy must have been crawling along as well. I looked out the windshield at the other truck and I could see they looked okay too. We opened our doors to get out and inspect the truck, but we did it cautiously, so as to avoid getting run over by the rest of the convoy as they rolled passed.

"What the hell were you doing on my side of the road?" asked the soldier from the other truck.

Sergeant T replied, "I wasn't even sure we were on the road."

We looked over both trucks. It looked like mangled bumpers and smashed hoods and radiators were the worst of the damage, a miracle in itself. Both trucks were still running. And, more importantly, the convoys on either side of us were still rolling, so we didn't waste any time.

Sergeant T started toward the driver's side door, but I got there first. "OH HELL NO," I said, climbing up into the driver's seat. "You're definitely not driving after that fiasco. We are lucky to be alive." It's true, we were fine—semi-trucks are pretty good armor—but it could have been a lot worse.

After hours of slow, tedious progress on the rough part of Route Tampa, we emerged from the blinding dust onto a four-lane highway that looked like any major highway in the southwest US. The expanse of the desert stretched on for miles with little or nothing to see. Every now and then we would pass someone on a bicycle and I'd wonder where they were coming from or where they were going.

Our convoy had just a few more miles to go before our only scheduled stop. Our trucks held about one hundred gallons of fuel, and by this point, pulling heavy loads over rough terrain, we'd burned about half of that. The sun was high in the sky and sweltering hot. We were bathed in dust and diesel exhaust, and I needed the bathroom. I could just make out the barricades of our fuel stop ahead as the convoy started to slow down. We parked our trucks outside the gate in a staggered parallel formation, so that each truck only had to defend one side of the convoy. The fuel stop was nothing more than a fenced-off section of highway that held an enormous makeshift fuel depot. This was the only point in the mission where we could get out of the truck in relative safety and relieve ourselves, but it wasn't like the whole convoy could fit inside the refueling stop, so most of us had to wait our turn outside the gates while fending off the hajis trying to sell us pirated DVDs, cigarettes, and booze.

I couldn't wait.

I grabbed my rifle, and a roll of toilet paper, and made my way to the back of the trailer. The axles on the back of the truck were close enough that the tires made a perfect toilet seat. I sat down, hunching over to get good and wedged in, without hitting my back on the trailer bed. I was just starting to pee, when a gaggle of Iraqi boys started wandering toward me. Shit, what are these guys doing? I quickly realized they were headed my way to sell me something. "Sergeant T! You need to help me here!"

I waved the roll of toilet paper around to warn them of what I was doing, but it seemed to have no effect. "Hey, stop! Can't you see that I'm going to the bathroom?" They didn't seem to understand what I was doing, and they even picked up their pace. They must have thought I was waving them over. I wasn't afraid of them—we had never had any trouble here—but I needed privacy.

SPC Decker, who was in the truck behind us, came running over, waving his rifle around. "Hey! Give the lady some privacy." His athletic build and booming voice got them to turn around quickly.

After I had finished, I went up to that group of Iraqis and showed them what the roll of toilet paper was used for. Not literally—I used mime. They all busted out into laughter. We didn't speak the same language, but the message was finally getting through. In this very rural part of Iraq, it may have been the first time these boys had ever seen toilet paper. I can guarantee you it was the first time they'd seen a woman miming going to the bathroom.

A year earlier, I couldn't have imagined I would have been sitting on the side of the road, in Iraq, miming to Iraqis what you do with toilet paper.

* * *

I could smell it in the air. We were close. At home, we were used to running water, electricity, and hygienic garbage disposal. We took these things for granted. But in Baghdad, the war had disrupted services as basic to human health as garbage collection, and I'm not sure those services were that well-established to begin with. In rural Iraq, those services had likely never existed in the first place. No matter where you were in Iraq, you were never very far from something disgusting. We'd be rolling through Baghdad and get a whiff of decay, and know that somewhere ahead of us was a mountain of garbage, just piled up in the street. No public cleanup services were coming. No street sweepers or recycling trucks. It was no wonder that the residents didn't even try to keep their city tidy. They were facing an impossible task. We had to deal with the disgusting fallout of that despair, and it made every convoy trip harder. And smellier.

By midafternoon, the hottest part of the day, people were starting to get tired of driving. After our rest stop, we'd been driving for another three hours. The convoy was well outside the city limits of Baghdad when I noticed that we were slowing down. *Oh, crap,* I thought, *someone must have blown a tire.* It wasn't an unusual occurrence—the heat was intense, and the tires had taken a beating on the earlier stretch of road. A blowout or two was almost inevitable. If it happened in a well-populated area, we'd usually keep driving, meaning that sometimes a tire would catch on fire. It could be scary, but a smoking tire wasn't worth putting the whole convoy in danger.

But this area didn't look too bad. The trucks came to a stop, everyone lining up in a herringbone formation. The formation made it so that any one of the trucks could escape if we came under attack, and it was easier to defend. I opened the passenger side door of my truck, weapon at low ready, trying to keep a low profile. We all knew what to do; we had done this many times before. I went to the front passenger tire and took up a low stance as we all defended the perimeter of the convoy, waiting while the tire was changed. The area we had stopped in wasn't exactly a city center, but it had some pedestrian traffic. As I scanned the passersby, I caught the eye of one woman, dressed entirely in black, with only her eyes visible. She looked into my eyes and I looked into hers. I can't imagine what must have been going through her head. I wondered if she yearned for the equal treatment that I enjoyed. Maybe she thought it was crazy and stupid to be doing the same thing as a guy.

I had seen how the Iraqi women were treated. They were the ones riding in the bed of the pickup trucks while the men drove; they were the ones working their asses off in the salt fields, while the men lay around and smoked. From my perspective, the women were treated more like property than people. I wondered what her life was like. I wondered if she had someone like Jake. Did people in this part of the world know love, like we did? Was it more of an arrangement for her? I wondered if seeing me doing my job made her question all the things she had been taught about women and their place in the world. We looked at each other for just a moment before she jerked her eyes away and continued on with whatever she was doing. I knew that our being here would probably not change the way she lived, but a small part of me wanted her to see what I was doing, and tell her daughters that they didn't have to live a life of servitude.

Moments later, we got the word to move out, and I made my way back into the truck, my weapon pointed out the window, not aiming at anyone in particular. We only had another hour or so to go before getting to Anaconda, and I was looking forward to being done for the day.

We finally made it to camp, and our convoy pulled into the unloading area. Unloading always took an hour or so. One by one, the trailers would pull up and the Conex boxes or pallets would be pulled off our trailers. Sitting and waiting, we could finally relax a little. I saw my reflection in the mirror of the truck; I looked like a wreck. My face was covered with dirt and sweat and my hair was matted from wearing my Kevlar all day. I peeled my flak vest off. Underneath, my T-shirt was soaked in sweat. I couldn't wait to get out of these clothes and get some real food in my stomach.

I looked for Jake's truck as we pulled into the chow hall parking lot. We usually met up here after being unloaded. Sergeant T and I made our way through the maze of vehicles. There was a fifty-five-gallon drum set up outside the chow hall, specifically for the purpose of clearing your rifle of chambered rounds, and I cleared mine before washing my hands in the basin by the door. As I was working the soap into my fingertips, I looked up in the mirror to see Jake smiling behind me.

"Still not going to wash your face, are you?" he said, still smirking. My filthy face had become a running joke with us. My sensitive skin was something we could both laugh at.

Going on a mission to Camp Anaconda meant getting to eat real food. I was looking forward to actual meat and real vegetables. As we stood in line, I told Jake about our trip up.

"So there I was, squatting on the tires . . ." I started.

"Okay, stop right there. We are in the chow hall. I don't want to hear any bathroom stories. Leave it for a letter home," he said. "I'm sure your family will get a kick out of it."

I liked the chow hall food more in theory than in actual practice, but we both grabbed a tray of whatever they were serving and sat down with a group of soldiers from our platoon. Sergeant T took a good ribbing for smashing up our truck, and we all relaxed as we ate.

No matter where we were, we loved the chow hall. It was where everyone came to sit back with a terrible cup of coffee, crack jokes, and speculate about whether the "ribs" the hall sometimes served were actually beef. It was here that the best stories got told, here that we had our deepest conversations, and here that we learned the most about who our battle buddies believed themselves to be. It was the social hub of the whole camp. We were under the illusion it was safe there, kind of. We could relax, away from the endless hardship of life outside.

Staying overnight in Anaconda was a different experience than Camp Cedar, because it was an active target for the enemy. Every night we spent there, we were sung to sleep by the too-close-for-comfort *thunk* of mortars shooting out of their tubes and sailing through the air toward the camp. The first few times were deeply nerve-wracking. We took a little comfort in the way the soldiers stationed there didn't seem concerned, though we still spent time fretting that sooner or later, one of the rounds would find its mark. After a while, even that fear became so much background noise. Eventually, we found the sound of the mortars soothing—the thud as one slid into the tube, the moment of silence, and then the muffled explosion as it landed in the dirt. We learned how to sleep soundly, even as the shots landed closer and closer to us, but . . . you know you're too comfortable with danger when mortars land near your compound and you roll over in bed, thinking, "That's way off. I've still got five minutes." If they got too close, we had small concrete bunkers to retreat to.

The next morning, I was awake for around thirty minutes before everyone got up. The mortars had started coming in again, as soon as there was a hint of light. It reminded me of the low rumble of thunder back home. In some ways, it was kind of like waking up to a thunderstorm rolling in off the cornfields. The mortars would start way off target, so all you would hear was a muffled boom in the distance, and then you would hear the sharp crack and feel the thunder of our return fire from the artillery battery stationed on base.

I reached over and nudged Jake. We all slept in one tent when we came up here.

"Hey, you awake?" I whispered looking for movement.

"I am now," he answered, clearly still sleepy.

"Shh. I have an idea, follow me." I waved him toward the tent flap.

We quietly made our way out of the tent. As soon as we were out of earshot, I pointed to a Conex box the mechanics were using as a garage. He got the idea pretty quickly and pulled me into his arms; our lips met as we disappeared into the shadows.

We snuck back to the tent just as people were waking up, and pretended to be packing and getting ready to head back to the trucks. Our trip back to Cedar always started with a stop at the chow hall, and then back to the freight yard to pick up the trailer—either empty or loaded up with stuff that had to go back south. We made our way out of base just as dawn broke and the sun filled the sky. We had twelve hours of driving ahead of us, and if everything went smoothly, we would pull into Cedar just as the sun set.

"Hey, why are we taking the New York Route?" I asked T as I followed the truck in front of me.

"Platoon Sargeant T said he got word before we left base that a convoy had been attacked on Tampa yesterday, just after we passed through."

I thought about that for a minute. "What do you mean, attacked? Did he give you any details?"

"Not much, just said that we weren't going to take Tampa for a while."

I wondered how bad an attack would have to be for the army to tell us to not take that route. I also wondered who would attack us. The people I see on the roads around here seem like they are having a hard enough time just getting by. I couldn't imagine that they'd have the resources and training to do something as dumb as attacking a heavily armed convoy full of redneck trigger-happy soldiers.

I glanced out the window. We were passing through a small town, with a little market that looked like something out of *Raiders of the Lost Ark*. Ramshackle carts carried everything from chickens to propane tanks, and market stands hawked fresh fruit and vegetables. I had no idea where they were getting this stuff. They certainly weren't growing it out in the desert.

As the truck hit another pothole in the road, I realized that I had an urgent need. I held on, hoping that the convoy would clear the town soon.

In this climate, it seemed like it got hotter every day. Just to deal with the heat, we had to drink copious amounts of water. I was on my second liter bottle of water for the day. My family had always teased me when I was a kid, calling me a camel because I never seemed to need a bathroom break. We'd go on day-long road trips to Minnesota and I'd never drink anything, so I'd never need a bathroom break. But here, in this camel-infested place, my own camel abilities were failing me.

"Sergeant T," I said as I tried to miss the next pothole that jumped out in front of us, "once we clear this town, you're going to have to take over driving."

"Sure, but we're going to have to do it while moving. You okay with that?"

I didn't have much choice. As we cleared the town, I looked over at Sergeant T and said, "You ready?"

"Sure, let's do it," he said, and reached for the wheel. The convoy picked up speed as we got clear of the local traffic. I kept my foot on the gas while he took control of the wheel, and I put my hands on the door latch. Sergeant T stood up, hunched over, and put one leg over the center console. I scooted over in my seat, cracking the door open to make room. My foot was still on the gas, but only by a hair. I opened the door wider, pushing hard against it with my shoulder to overcome the pressure of the wind. Sergeant T was almost completely over on the driver's side, ready for the switch. My foot left the gas. The truck decelerated almost instantly, and I felt my momentum carry me forward. Just as I caught myself, his foot recovered the throttle position and the momentum switched the other way. The truck was moving again. I slipped out of the door, still fighting the wind, and started for the catwalk.

I tried not to look down. Below me, the road was rushing past at fifty miles per hour. Hanging on to the side of a moving truck, I was extra careful with my footing. Hand over hand, I made my way around the cab, heading for the catwalk. Once there, I was on steady ground, or as steady as one could be on a semi-truck barreling down the highway. I looked left and right, and dang it, there were more people around. I thought we were clear of that little city. What were these people doing out here?

I waited for a just a few more seconds. How many people could be wandering around out in the desert? I finally got to a point where I couldn't see anyone, and decided to get it over with.

Here's a little tip, learned the hard way: if you ever pee off a moving vehicle, make sure you don't pee into the wind.

Thinking about it now, these tricks seem terrifying. The number of times I could have died just in the course of trying to pee seems astronomical. I would never try these maneuvers in the civilian world. That said, at the time, they seemed completely normal. Inevitable, really. Realistically, the problems we faced on the road could only be solved through these unconventional methods.

This is one of the hardest things for civilians to grasp about military life: the way your expectations change is gradual, but complete. You get used to things that civilians see as completely strange. Things as crazy as peeing through a catwalk grate as your truck hurtles down the highway become just part of your day. Driving around a population center, nudging cars off the road while pointing rifles out your truck cab's window feels like the only sensible way to operate. The things that feel normal while you're in the military are completely contrary to the things that feel normal at home. It's no wonder that soldiers have such a hard time easing back into civilian life. The foundations of what they think of as reasonable and decent have completely shifted, usually so thoroughly that the soldier can't really conceive of any other way to think.

Pulling into Camp Cedar was always a triumphant occasion. We'd made one more full trip, delivered supplies to soldiers who needed them, and now, as a reward, we got a day of no more driving. To top it all off, we came home with all the same people we'd left with. We parked the trucks in the motor pool as the sun set. I couldn't wait to meet up with Jake.

"You'll never guess what I did today," I said, smiling as he approached.

"Do I even want to know? Did it involve the bathroom?"

I gave him a little shove. "Stop it! You totally want to hear this." I told him all about my adventure on the catwalk as we made our way back to the tent and our honeymoon suite. As it turns out, this switcheroo became a pretty regular thing. It became known as "The Catwalk Maneuver."

The next day it was hot enough to melt tarmac. Dry and dusty, the sky a sort of distant haze. My post was at the top of this old ammo bunker in the shape of a pyramid on the outskirts of camp. To get to the top, you scrambled up a narrow zigzag path, dirt shifting under your boots, certain that at any moment you could lose your balance and topple back down the hill.

At the top of the bunker was a little lookout shelter, covered in a flapping layer of ponchos to keep the sun off any sad soldiers who were stuck up there for the day. Our platoon leader had pulled two women to do this duty while giving us no form of communication. Specialist Proggins and I hunkered down in the shade, our rifles by our sides, and started the slow process of getting through the day. But as we watched the seemingly unchanging desert horizon, we spotted two guys, dressed in scruffy tan robes, driving a herd of camels through the empty desert. They were tiny on the horizon, but they were getting bigger. Definitely headed our way.

"What do we do if they get too close?" Proggins asked.

"I suppose we yell at them first, and then start shooting." As eager as I was to get into some fighting, I was not interested in shooting two innocent camel herders.

These guys were literally in the middle of nowhere, nothing but sand as far as the eye could see. I couldn't imagine where they'd come from or where they were headed, but the fact that they were out there made them a threat. We had signs all around the camp that warned people to keep back and stay away or be shot, in both English and Arabic. You had to be a complete moron to get close. So, yeah. They looked suspicious. We had our rifles locked and loaded. All the same, I was really hoping we wouldn't have to shoot anyone. I thought to myself, *Sure would be nice to have a radio.* And I hoped my rifle marksmanship wouldn't steer me wrong if I needed to use it.

We lay absolutely still, watching them approach through the sights on our rifles. Closer. Closer. My hands grew sweatier. I tried to keep my breath even, knowing that my marksmanship depended on keeping my body still, but my heart was beating like a hummingbird.

But they didn't see us. They didn't even care about the camp. The men walked past and the camels followed. Thank God we didn't have to shoot them.

Looking back, they could have easily just been scouting the place out for later, but that possibility was the furthest thing from my mind. I looked at Proggins, and said, "That was a relief."

"You're telling me!" she said. We spent the rest of the day joking about what the odds were that we would end up eating one of the camels we'd just seen in the chow hall someday. It was the first time I really spent one on one with Proggins. I realized that because I had Jake with me, I wasn't really leaning on my relationships with the other women in the company. I wondered if Jake was the same way. Were we not forming the same kind of bonds that others were starting to form with one another?

In the evening, we'd sit around with our friends on folding camp chairs, chatting, maybe listening to music, comparing stories about our childhood, and fantasizing about the comfort food of our homes. Most of our company was Native American or Hispanic, and raised in the Southwest. Their backgrounds and perspectives were nothing like mine or Jake's, but when you're stuck with people for months on end, all the usual barriers start to break down.

It was during these evenings when we gathered around talking that I realized what the difference was. I kept comparing the bond that Jake and I were forming with the bond that we were all forming as a platoon. It was different and the same, because while it was built on trying times and the need to rely on each other, Jake and I knew we would be together after this was over. I sometimes felt bad for the people in my company. I could see the longing they felt for their loved ones. I could see the way they looked at Jake and me when we had a momentary lapse of discretion and slipped into husband and wife mode. I could see how the distance and the time away from loved ones had already taken their toll. I realized that it wasn't the long, hot days, the constant anxiety, or the terrible food and living conditions that made this war hard on them. It was being away from their family, from home, and from everything familiar that made all of this worse. I had the one thing that made all of that absence and distance irrelevant: my husband.

The days came and went. The pony express never stopped. The routine became automatic. We knew when we would have to go out. We knew what routes we would take. Heck, we even knew some of the *haji* salespeople at the refueling stop by name. I would take my turn driving in the morning—either to or from Anaconda—and my partner would take the afternoon. Switching drivers was like clockwork, and afterwards, I'd settle in for an afternoon nap.

And then it happened.

CHAPTER 16

The Day It Got Real

Midafternoon in early July 2003, just south of Al Diwaniyah, Iraq. The sun was blazing in a sweltering blue sky, and there was nothing but sand for as far as I could see. Four hours into our mission, we were rolling down the highway, pulling a trailer loaded up with Conex boxes. The heat was immense, so I'd taken my flak vest off and set it by my side, next to my rifle. I tried to make myself comfortable, but sweat was dripping down my face. My legs and combat boots were up on the dash and I had my hands behind my head, all set for as much of a nap as I could get before it was my turn to drive. My codriver had everything under control.

POP-POP-POP-POP! I jumped out of my slumber, as I felt and heard the truck accelerate. "What the hell is going on?" I shouted, coming awake with a massive breath that made my voice squeak. "What tire did we blow? All of them?" One

189

look at SGT Nez and I knew we hadn't blown a tire. He'd gone pale (which, considering his Native American ancestry, was quite a feat). His hands gripped the steering wheel with a white-knuckle intensity.

"We're being attacked," he managed. If I hadn't heard the gunshots, I might have thought he was joking. It was like I'd asked him, "What color is the sky?" and he'd replied, "It's blue of course," with little to no emotion in his response. I know it seems odd, but I was a little stunned at first. Here I was in Iraq, in the middle of a war zone, and I was *stunned* that someone was shooting at us. I think maybe I thought it just wouldn't happen because it hadn't yet, or maybe everyone feels this way the first time they get shot at. It took me about half a second to process, and then my eyes darted around the cab, looking for my flak vest and rifle. My heart rate instantly doubled, and I could almost feel the adrenaline pulsing through my veins.

Outside, a cloud of dust and smoke had surrounded us. Zero visibility. I didn't know where I should aim, but I scrambled for my rifle, got it in position, locked and loaded, pulled the trigger and . . .

"Shit! My rifle is jammed!" I shouted, and knew instantly months of sandstorms and a lack of maintenance had come back to screw me. I cursed myself under my breath. Nez didn't even acknowledge me, his fists still in a death grip on the steering wheel, his foot as far down on the pedal as it could go.

I'd never really believed that I'd have to use it, and now the inside of my rifle was saturated with sand. I had no defense. Our only prayer was to keep going and get through the patch of enemy fire.

That couldn't be our only option. It just couldn't. I slammed the assist on my rifle and cycled a round out that flew off behind the seat. I still couldn't see anything, but as I scrabbled at my rifle, I heard a much bigger impact. I didn't know what it was, but I knew it was not a rifle round that I had just heard. The smoke was getting thicker, and I still couldn't shoot.

The strangest thing, looking back on that first attack, was that I wasn't scared at all, except for that initial split second of realization. I felt an intense spike of fear that almost instantly turned into rage. I kept working on my rifle, beating the shit out of it, trying to get it to fire, ejecting round after round, hoping one would go off. I was furious that I couldn't shoot back. The seconds felt like minutes. It was like everything was in slow motion, but the whole fight lasted probably less than thirty seconds.

As the smoke cleared I could hear the QRF (Quick Reaction Force) trucks. They must have just rolled up on the ambush site. Behind us, we heard a cacophony of machine gunfire —the 50cal and the grenade launchers mounted on the trucks—and then it was silent. That's when I started scanning my body. Patting up and down my legs and torso. They say that people can be shot and not even know it, so a full body check is actually necessary. I looked over at Nez, to see if I could see any obvious wounds. Nothing.

"Are you okay?" I asked, sucking in a breath.

"Yeah, I think so. You think we are all clear? Or could there be more?" His eyes were still glued to the truck in front of us.

"There better not be, my rifle is useless."

We got through a few more miles, until we were outside the kill zone. As soon as my adrenaline-induced rage subsided, I thought of Jake. I know it sounds weird, but I wasn't panicked with concern. I hoped he was okay—I wanted to know he was okay—but I knew that I couldn't just get out of the truck, abandon Nez and my duties, and go find him. I knew that if he was hurt, I was not the person who would be best able to help him. I knew that I had things to do here and now, and God forbid, if something did happen, someone from my platoon would come find me. It was kind of an unspoken agreement. If we were apart, people would pass messages for us, just quick verbal things like "Jake made it up to Anaconda okay" or "Jake asked me to tell you . . ." It was as if people understood that even though we kept everything very professional on the surface, underneath we were always eager to hear something from or about one another.

The convoy pulled over. We got out, walked around—I kept an eye on the horizon in case the enemy had decided to give chase—and made sure that the truck was still functional. As I walked the length of the trailer looking for damage, I could see smoke pouring out of Skinny's truck, just behind us. I rushed to the cab. Luckily, the smoke was coming from the Conex box (thank God) on the back of his trailer, not the cab. I shouted into the cab, "Skinny, are you guys okay?" The cab door opened and revealed bullet holes in the side of the truck. Skinny climbed out of the cab, looking pale.

"Yeah, I think so," he mumbled. "I think I got shot."

"What? I just asked if you were okay. If you got shot, you're NOT okay."

He pointed to his arm. A bullet had hit some part of the cab, ricocheted, and gone clean through his bicep. His codriver had been hit too, just a graze, but he still looked pretty shaken up. The QRF Humvee pulled up, and SGT Ball, our combat medic, jumped out, already carrying his gear, and rushed over to Skinny.

Everything after that was kind of a blur. The medics patched up Skinny, letting him sit and apply pressure to his wounds, on a cot, as they tended to everyone else who had been injured. A few RPG rounds had hit the truck just in front of mine, and Skinny's truck just behind me. They'd shot up trucks up and down the convoy as well, but it seemed like they'd completely missed ours.

It was as the chopper took off, my wounded brothers safely inside, that I felt Jake's hand on my shoulder. He asked if I was okay, and then asked about Skinny. He knew Skinny had been shot, but Jake didn't know how bad it was. "Weirdly enough," he said, smiling, "we didn't even realize the convoy was under attack until we stopped."

It was a wakeup call for all of us. Until now, we had all been acting as if this was an extended annual training event. All National Guard soldiers spend two weeks per year training with their unit, doing whatever job it is that their unit does. Sometimes the conditions are rough, forcing us to set up tents and camp out, not too dissimilar to what we were doing now. The general idea was that you trained with your unit to maintain and improve your skill level. Until now that's really how it felt in Iraq; one big simulated training mission. Now everything had changed. We were at war, and now, everyone felt it.

A few days later we were plowing down the highway, trying to get to Baghdad as quickly as possible. I was riding again, with Koster driving, and we had Nelly's "Hot In Herre" playing on the cheapo boom box that we had bungee corded to the dash. It was the irony of this song that made it one of our favorites. I couldn't really hear it over the roar of the engine and the hairdryer-like wind blowing in on us, but that didn't matter. I was looking out the window; my rifle tracking my sight, cleaned and ready. I had spent nearly all of our day in-between that last mission and this one cleaning my rifle. When I'd disassembled it, I'd been appalled at how much dirt and sand had collected in the most critical parts. I had no intention of getting caught again with no way to defend myself apart from throwing water bottles out the window. There was a part of me that was still hoping that last mission was a fluke, maybe some wack job ex-Republican Guard who'd crawled out of his hole to take vengeance. But I didn't think that was true. And I had a round locked and loaded.

We were passing through a tiny town, not much more than a few ramshackle buildings in the middle of the desert. Some women were working in the field, and a few children were huddled together next to a building. As the convoy approached, the kids ran up to the side of the road, hands high in the air, open with a gesture asking for treats. I tossed out an MRE to one, careful to get it far from the trucks, far enough that they wouldn't get run over. A few of them scrambled out to get it. And out of nowhere, I heard shots. The kids scattered, running back toward the building. The women in the field dropped their baskets and ran back toward the buildings. Everyone knew what was coming.

I couldn't see anyone shooting at us, but I could hear it over the engine, which meant it was probably close. The convoy kept moving. I didn't hear any return fire, so presumably no one knew where it was coming from, but the convoy picked up speed. Koster pushed his foot to the floor to keep up, and I saw our QRF truck racing back down the road, looking for the source. We heard more rounds, and saw a few hit the pavement, but still had no idea where it was coming from. We were surrounded by kids and obviously innocent people. We couldn't just lay down suppressive fire.

A few miles outside the town, the convoy pulled over to check on the trucks and to make sure no one was injured. This was the second mission in a row that our convoy had been attacked, and we were all on high alert. We formed our makeshift perimeter and started looking over the trucks for damage. Luckily no one had been hit this time, but the Conex box on the back of Jake's trailer had been shot up. I was only one truck in front of Jake and SGT Kuna. We always tried to stick close to each other when we could. Moreover, Kuna and Koster were poker buddies, and liked to pick up a quick game at the refueling stop while we waited for the rest of the convoy. Jake opened up the Conex box to make sure nothing inside was on fire. This was one of the things we'd been warned against: a tracer round could find its way in, light something on fire, and then you'd be hauling a burning trailer down the road at fifty miles per hour.

"Hey, come check this out," Jake called as he opened the Conex box doors.

Kuna, Koster, and I trotted toward the back of the trailer. As I rounded the corner, I found Jake sporting a desert camo vest—a vest that was substantially better than the Vietnam-era flak vests we were all wearing. Kuna and Koster climbed into the box. Kuna picked one up and read its description. His eyes went wide. "These are fuckin' bulletproof vests! Brand new!" Kuna was already sliding his arm into one. "And here we are, getting all shot up in these forty-year-old flak vests that probably wouldn't stop a rock kicked up from the tires on Tampa."

"Heidi, try this one on," Jake said, handing me a vest. It fit perfectly. A little heavy, due to the ceramic plates that made it actually bulletproof, but I was happy to have it on.

"Go wave down the QRF truck," Koster said, as he grabbed a few of them. If anyone needed these, it was the QRF guys. The truck pulled up, and we discreetly handed them a dozen or so vests. I could see the gratitude in their eyes as they put them on. It was only the second time we had really been under fire, but something told us it wouldn't be the last. The army did eventually get around to issuing these to the whole unit, but until it did, our little group had a spare set.

Things were changing for everyone. The insurgents, as we were now calling them, were starting to get their act together. They were executing ambushes all over Iraq. Because of our vulnerability, convoys like ours were huge targets. We were essentially driving civilian trucks painted green, and all we had for support was what we could mount on a Humvee. The insurgents quickly learned that they could cause massive amounts of damage with roadside bombs (later known as IEDs), which changed the face of the whole war. The tempo was picking up. From that first ambush on, we rarely ran a mission without taking enemy fire.

But, as their tactics grew more brutal, our defenses became more efficient.

We'd almost reached the rear entrance of the Baghdad Airport when I briefly heard some automatic fire, and the entire median of the highway exploded for what seemed like half a mile. As smoke and dust filled the air, I felt my truck lean to one side. Time slowed as I felt the side of my truck rise into the air, hesitate, and then fall again. On the way down, I heard an intense ringing noise in my ears, a noise that kept getting louder and sharper. I looked over at Decker and tried to speak. *Are you okay?* But I couldn't hear myself. I knew my mouth was moving, and I knew words were coming out, but I couldn't hear anything. I could see Decker going through the same motions. The convoy had completely stopped. Dust and smoke flooded the air, so thick you couldn't see anything around the truck, and the overpass just in front of us was completely obscured.

The drivers of the truck that was just in front of the overpass as the ambush began had the forethought to stop. Maybe it was the shock of the blast or the fact that they couldn't see anything that had spurred them to make that decision. We were at the tail end of the convoy; most of the trucks had made it beneath the overpass, but they might have been attacked on the other side. No way to see. We got out of the truck, weapons ready, looking for a target. I remembered that, just before the explosion, I'd heard a bunch of automatic fire, so I knew someone was also shooting at us. But now, because of the smoke, I couldn't see anything, and because of the explosion, I couldn't hear anything.

Up until this attack, every time we'd been ambushed, it had been at fifty miles per hour, with a brief period in the kill zone. Maybe we'd return fire, but we'd always been able to accelerate away. Here, we'd been forced to stop in the middle of the kill zone. We had to get out of our trucks and fight. I gave Decker a look: *we might as well get out, we're sitting ducks here.* He opened his door, I opened mine, and we both opened fire. I knew someone was out there, and I wasn't going to give them an open shot on me.

The dust and smoke cleared a bit, and we could make out a little farm and a mud-stone house. In front was one of the typical *haji* orange and white pickup trucks. It was the only place someone could hide, so I fired in that direction. I took what little cover I could just behind the front tire of my truck. I still couldn't hear anything, so I was looking for muzzle flashes from the dark recesses of the windows. I saw something, in the top window, just a quick burst, but undoubtedly muzzle flashes. I think I must have emptied a whole magazine into that window.

I looked over, peeking my head around the tire, to check on the truck behind me. I had just loaded a fresh magazine, and I saw Jake looking my way. His truck was right behind mine in the convoy. He gave me a nod, and I turned my attention back to the little farmhouse in front of us, and I thought *this is one hell of a honeymoon.* The smoke wasn't quite clear, and I still couldn't see under the overpass. So I just kept shooting, trying to be selective now, because I had already gone through two full magazines.

From the corner of my eye, I saw the truck in front of us begin to move. My hearing was beginning to return, little by little, and I hoped Decker's was as well. "Decker! Let's get the hell out of here." I hoped he could hear me. I saw him move toward the driver's door, and I made a move toward the passenger door, still firing, hoping that if there were still people in that building, they were keeping their head down. I glanced back and saw Jake and Kuna doing the same thing.

The tail end of our convoy headed out as fast as our trucks would take us. We turned into the back entrance of the airport just a few miles up the road from the ambush site. The rest of the convoy had been parked just inside the perimeter, waiting for us.

"Holy crap," I said, as Jake approached. "That was *intense.*"

"Yeah, it was like the whole side of the road just rose into the air in slow motion. When we jumped out, I saw you empty your whole magazine into the farmhouse. I figured you could take care of yourself after seeing that."

It was the first time we'd actually known where the shots were coming from, and we were able to return the favor. We were all pretty high on adrenaline. I don't think any of us spared a thought for how close we'd come to being blown up. That was a massive IED.

It's bad to think about battle too much, but the rush you get is almost addictive. In the heat of battle, I never actually thought about the possibility that I could die. The adrenaline started pumping and the only thing that went through my mind was causing as much damage as possible and taking out whoever was trying to kill us. Even when we were under attack, my mind wasn't thinking about Jake or the fact that I could be injured; it was only thinking about where to shoot next. I suppose this was the point of basic training—to drill those reactions in so deeply that you don't even think about them, you just move from one target to the next. That's the essence of fight or flight. You do what you have to do. When it was all over, that's when I could think about my husband.

Ambushes and firefights grew more and more common during our time in Camp Cedar. Every time we went out, we knew we could be attacked. We knew it might be the last time we saw each other. We dealt with that stress by focusing on the details of the potential attack, sometimes placing bets or using other guessing games to keep ourselves focused on the road and the possibility of battle: "Maybe it'll be under that piece of garbage." Or, "Maybe they'll come from that hut there." Thinking about it now, we were dealing with an enormous amount of stress. Making it into a game worked for us.

Being fired on became so commonplace that we stopped being all that concerned whenever we heard shots. On one occasion, when I was partnered with Skinny, we saw rounds hitting the road in front of us, and I could faintly hear the shots being fired in the distance over the rumble of the exhaust. I had no idea where they were coming from.

"You see that?" I asked, scanning the houses in the distance for muzzle flashes.

"Yeah." Skinny was a man of few words. He didn't seem all that concerned, and to be honest, neither was I. This happened a lot. You could tell the convoy was taking fire, but we were in a highly populated part of Baghdad and you couldn't see where it was coming from.

"Think I should do anything about it?" I couldn't see any hostile targets, but sometimes we would pop off a few rounds in the direction of fire in hopes it would scare them away. This was easy to do in the more rural areas, but not so much in a populated urban center. Too many innocent bystanders.

"No, why bother? They won't hit us. They never do." The insurgents were amazingly bad at precision fire, and usually too chicken to get close enough to our convoys to do much damage.

"Yeah, you're right," I said. "It's not like you've ever been shot, or anything." We couldn't get too worked up, but it was frustrating, not being able to shoot back at a visible target.

This shift in thinking took place without me really noticing it. I think it was the same way for everyone. When something happens often enough, all of the sudden it becomes normal. For us, this was IEDs and ambushes. It wasn't like it had been in the beginning, when we were lax and unprepared, but still at ease with it. Now, if anything, we were overprepared. We had taken our old flak vests and zip tied them to the inside of our cab, looking for some resistance to the shrapnel. We'd armored our Humvees with scrap metal and set sandbags on the hoods of the trucks up near the windshields for cover. In just a few short weeks, we'd gone from playing soldier to being battle-hardened vets.

Whenever we left the relative safety of the bases, our attitudes changed. We noticed things in more detail, scrutinizing everything, something called situational awareness. Did that patch of ground look like it had been dug up? Was that guy on the overpass just crossing the highway, or was he scouting us out? Was that car trying to nudge its way into the convoy going to blow up? We would notice even small details about things that were wrong with our trucks: low tires, loose bolts, etc. . . . Everything was a potential threat. It wasn't fear. It's not like we left the base and felt the way you do when you almost get into a car accident, or when a bear is charging at you. It was more anticipation, knowing that at any moment the whole course of your life could change.

As we drew closer to September, our six-month deployment in Iraq was close to finishing. Rumors were going around that we might be going home soon.

But one afternoon in formation, when we were all expecting to hear about our assignments for the mission the next day, Top delivered some different information.

"I have news for everyone," he said. "I know our orders were for a six-month deployment, and a lot of you are expecting to go home soon. I have just gotten word from the captain that our orders have been revised and we will be staying for a full year."

You could have heard a pin drop. Everyone was in shock; it was the exact opposite of the news we had been expecting. I almost felt sick. I couldn't imagine another six months here. The first six had been difficult enough. Even though Jake and I had each other, our own antidotes to loneliness and the stress of war, I wanted to get back home and get on with our lives. I had been daydreaming about what we would do when we returned: fantasies of road trips without having to look for IEDs, and the kind of sand that was next to an ocean. They were what I clung to when I needed something to keep me going. I knew I couldn't dwell on it; we had no choice, we were soldiers. This is what soldiers do. They suck it up and drive on.

The mission the next day started off in a somber mood. The usual banter was missing, as were the usual makin'-it-work smiles on soldiers' faces. Koster and I just got up in our truck and did our thing. It was just after we stopped for fuel and lunch, while the convoy was rolling as fast as we dared down the middle of the highway, that an IED went off, just ahead of our truck. I felt it almost as much as I heard it. From that mission on, I always knew how far ahead Jake's truck was. The days of casual certainty were over.

CHAPTER 17

The Times They Are a-Changin'

"Hurry up! If you want to be first in line, we've got to leave now!" Jake was climbing up into the cab of our bobtail (a semi cab without a trailer). When we were back in camp, Jake and I used his truck, and Koster and Kuna used my truck.

I tossed my rifle in the box behind the cab, and closed the padlock on it. In Camp Cedar, we didn't always carry our rifles. As I slid around to the passenger side and into the cab, I remembered Top's warning about the new colonel.

"Okay, now remember: you can't go tearing down the road kicking up dust like you always do. The new colonel will have a fit."

As I closed the door, I felt Jake accelerate and fishtail out of the motor pool, and I knew we were headed for trouble. He knew if we weren't first in line, my hunger would set in, and he was more comfortable getting chewed out by a colonel then dealing with me waiting for food. As we sped down the road, a rooster tail of dust kicking up behind us, I saw a Humvee in the side mirror approaching quickly.

"Um, you might want to slow down," I said as I made out who was driving the Humvee. And then the truck lurched, like we'd hit the biggest pothole in the world.

"What the hell was that?" Jake started slowing down, thinking something might have happened to the truck. We all drove a little crazy when we didn't have a trailer attached; it was the one way we could blow off a little steam, especially when we were in the relative safety of camp.

The driver of the Humvee must have already known about the new speed bumps. It was nearly impossible to see them in the fading light, and Jake had hit one way too fast. As Jake pulled the bobtail to a careful crawl, the Humvee pulled up next to us. Inside, the new colonel was waving at us to stop and pull over.

"I frickin' told you so," I said as the colonel jumped up on the running boards of the truck and started yelling at us.

"What the hell is your problem, Specialist?" shouted the Colonel. "I put out a new order yesterday, a five-mile-per-hour speed limit around camp. You had to be going thirty, at least."

"We weren't here yesterday," Jake said, all innocence, knowing that the colonel wouldn't care about the details. "We just pulled into camp an hour ago."

The colonel yelled at us for a few more minutes, threatening all kinds of hell and paperwork. Jake just sat and listened, nodding appropriately, trying to hold back a sly smirk. I was giving him that *I told you so* stare. As the colonel jumped down from our truck, Jake looked back at me and said, "Don't worry, I'll get him back."

"Sure you will, babe."

At least the line for the chow hall moved quickly. It was nice to finally have a legit chow hall at Camp Cedar. We had gotten used to it in Camp Anaconda, and now we had one at both camps. It was the simple things, like having a real chow hall, that made life a little easier on us. It gave us more time to spend with our fellow soldiers, enjoying each other's camaraderie and telling our "war" stories from the last mission.

When we finally left the hall, last as usual—eating here was the high point of my day, so we relished it as long as we could—I hopped back into Jake's cab, ready to go back to our tents. I had nearly forgotten the evening's altercation with the colonel. But Jake hadn't.

"Don't worry," he said, as he put the truck into gear. "This time I'll follow all the rules and drive incredibly slow."

Somehow, I didn't think that would happen. He pulled away and much to my surprise, he drove well below the five-mile-per-hour rule. His truck was barely crawling down the little road that circled camp.

"I see what you're doing here," I said, knowing all too well what he was trying to do. "Killing them with kindness, eh?" I looked behind us and saw that same Humvee, tail-gaiting us. It looked as though he was gesturing so I squinted to make out what he was doing. "Jake! That's the dang colonel behind us! He's throwing his fists up in the air. I think he's pissed at you for driving too slow."

"Too slow, too fast. I wish he'd make up his mind. He did say he didn't want to see my truck kicking up any more dust. I'm just following orders. I told you I'd get him back."

* * *

For six months, we had been living in Camp Cedar in primitive conditions, and now, on the other side of camp, near the new chow hall, contractors were busy setting up more civilized accommodations for us. I wasn't sure how I felt about this. Don't get me wrong: newer, better amenities were always going to be newer and better. But by this time, we had acclimated. It was still ungodly hot, but my body no longer complained about the heat, like it had when we'd first arrived. In those first few weeks, it was a matter of seconds before the intense heat would zap the energy from my body. Now, it took much longer for that to happen. I knew how to cope with it before getting exhausted. And now that our bodies had become acclimated to the cruel Iraqi heat, we had contractors installing a new tent city, with industrial air-conditioning units. I felt like all that suffering had been for nothing.

It was a bit like watching our old primitive tent site get taken down: bittersweet. We had built that site up, from scratch, as a unit, with our own blood, sweat, and tears. Jake and I had spent countless nights under the stars, falling asleep, side by side. Was that changing too?

Everything was replaced with something newer and better suited to the environment. The new tents were canvas, with raised plywood floors to keep out the sand and bugs, and instead of the folding army cots, everyone got a proper bed. But the most important change was the air conditioners. Big enough to cool an apartment building, powerful enough that you needed a heavy-duty blanket to keep warm at night. During the day, they brought the temperature in the tents down to a perfectly civilized eighty-five degrees. We hadn't been this cool in months.

The contractors also took down the old ramshackle showers (which was great, but made it impossible for us to shower together anymore) and latrines and replaced them with real facilities, complete with running water. The new bathrooms were all on trailers—and the limits on how many showers you could take were gone. I could brush my teeth and wash my face in a sink with a mirror instead of trying to get it all done under a yellowing plastic water bottle. We also got access to a laundry service, meaning that our Laura Ingalls Wilder days were over. The only thing we needed to do for laundry was pass it to whoever had laundry duty that week, and it would get run through a proper washing machine.

It wasn't like the new civilizing facilities could fix *everything*: we were still dealing with the reality of living out in the Iraqi desert. We still had brutal sandstorms that covered literally everything, even the stuff inside the tents, with a fine layer of dirt and sand that revealed the persistent presence of kangaroo rats and other creepy-crawlies. Paw prints everywhere. I'd be grossed out if I hadn't already gotten used to it.

And no matter how civilized camp got, we still had to leave every few days to do the pony express. The roads were more dangerous than ever before. IEDs were everywhere, ambushes were more frequent. But the new luxuries we had at camp at least made the downtime in-between missions more relaxing—and removed the need for some of the more laborious duties.

And every good thing has a price. The new air conditioning meant that our bodies, previously acclimated to the desert heat and misery, started complaining again whenever we went outside. We got soft. But worse than that, with the new tents came new, stricter rules. Our old sleeping arrangements were no longer approved of, and Jake and I had to bunk separately—Jake with the guys, and me with the other women. I instantly missed falling asleep wrapped up in Jake's arms, so whenever we weren't on a mission, I spent all my time in Jake's tent, snuggled under the covers with him. I worried a little that my presence might make Jake's tent mates uncomfortable, but they never said anything about it. The more time I spent over there, the more they came to see me as just one of the guys. And Jake and I still found time to be alone.

One evening, as I was walking back from the shower trailer, I ran into SSGT Macheco.

"Hey, Radkiewicz, there's a five-ton parked out in front of our tents. Would you make sure it gets back to the motor pool tonight?"

"Sure thing," I said, and I dropped off my stuff in my tent before heading over to Jake's place.

"Hey, is everyone decent in there?" I shouted. In a tent, there are no doors, so shouting is the politest way to announce yourself. I heard a muffled reply. Taking it as an affirmative, I ducked and opened the tent flap, and made my way inside.

The inside of the tents was light green, with a repeating boho pattern that made them feel very Middle Eastern. The guys had "decorated" with uniforms, towels, and other knick-knacks hanging from the walls, and what looked like a prayer rug in the center of the room. Along one wall sat a few MRE cases that supported their only form of entertainment, a nine-inch DVD player that managed to keep working, despite the dust. In the evening, or on downtime between missions, we'd put on a movie, and I would hang out and watch them on Jake's bed with the rest of his squad.

I found Jake organizing his footlocker. "Hey, do you want to come with me? Macheco told me to put that five-ton back in the motor pool." Jake's eyes lit up.

"Sure, let's go." He laced up his boots in a hurry. As we left the tent, the guys gave us a little flak about my choice in battle buddies—gentle teasing that made me feel at home. Jake and I got to the truck, hopped inside, and drove it over to the motor pool. I found a spot in the back, parked it and was beginning to lock it up when it occurred to me that we were all alone. It was late at night, we didn't have a mission, and we were off duty, so . . . we figured we'd "take our time" getting back to the tents. Since we now had to sleep in different tents, we had to be a little more strategic and creative about making time for one another.

The improvements to the new camp didn't stop with construction. We got signed up for a convoy-training course in Kuwait and some new weapons training. No one had explained exactly what type of training we would receive, but we figured that it was always valuable to learn new things, and at least it would give us a bit of a break from running missions up to Anaconda. Mostly we were just excited to get out of Iraq for a little while. We weren't particular about the reason why.

We convoyed down and across the border into Kuwait, driving without trailers this time, and arriving at the training facility without incident. As we crossed the border, I remembered my initial anxiety about driving into a war zone, and I laughed a little at how innocent I'd been. It was rare now that we'd run a mission without having to exchange fire with the enemy, and I was just as badass at laying down suppressive fire as any of the people in my unit.

Once we arrived, we realized that the "facility" part of "training facility" was more of a wish than a reality. It consisted of a single canvas tent, a few benches, and four guys assigned to train us. This place was almost as bare bones as Camp Cedar had been when we first arrived. The instructors set up a half-hour PowerPoint presentation on "How to Drive in a Convoy During Combat," which made a couple of us burst into laughter. We did try to be respectful, but we'd been convoying in combat conditions for a while now, and it was pretty obvious these guys were amateurs compared to us. The "training" itself was laughably beneath our abilities. The time to train us in that skill was before the enemy started shooting at us, not after.

The saddest part about this trip was that these four guys hadn't known what our experiences had been like. They were genuinely expecting a troop of newbies to show up, all flustered and frightened by the thought of a Haji with an AK. When they realized they were wasting our time, and therefore their time, they were quick to apologize, and ask for our advice on what we had learned from our experiences. We had a little bit of fun turning the tables and schooling these guys on what combat was like for us.

But whatever. We were already a day away from camp. The trip down to the "training facility" was another chance for us to flout the tighter accommodation rules: we spent the night on the hood of our truck (which I was slightly uneasy about, fearing that I'd roll off the hood in the middle of the night), looking at the stars, curled against each other, just as we had when we'd first arrived in this part of the world.

The next day was devoted to weapons training, universally valuable. Everyone, even the most experienced marksman, can benefit from an afternoon of driving around a course and trying to shoot at cardboard bad guys. Jake was in extra need of that practice time: the week before, he had run over his rifle with his truck in an early-morning, bleary-eyed accident, and had been issued a new rifle that he needed to sight. We spent the whole day gleefully shooting (knowing that they weren't shooting back) and chasing down cardboard targets.

We said our goodbyes to the instructors who turned out to be pretty nice guys after all, then began to head back to Camp Cedar. We got about an hour down the road when we saw a pair of Humvees blocking the highway near the border crossing, so the lead truck made a left into the nearby base on the Kuwait-Iraq border. When we pulled in and got out of the trucks, we learned that the border had just closed. No one was saying why. We resigned ourselves to spending a few extra days here, with nothing to do except pass the time. Our platoon sergeant snagged a tent for us all to stay in, and told us to keep out of trouble and be ready to go in the morning in case the border reopened earlier than expected.

A few of us decided to roam around and see what the camp had to offer. We found all sorts of luxuries that we didn't have up in Camp Cedar or Anaconda. There was a tent full of computers connected to the internet and an aspiring Kuwaiti entrepreneur who charged $10 an hour to use them. They had a phone tent, and I made a mental note to make sure to call home later that evening after chow. Trying to figure what time it was back home was always a challenge, but I knew the later I called, the better. Then I saw a little trailer that looked like a PX but had some Arabic writing on the sign outside.

"Hey Jake, let's go check that place out," I said, as I grabbed his hand and tugged him after me. We got inside and saw all sorts of jewelry. And it got me thinking: we were coming up on our first anniversary.

It was amazing how much of a whirlwind the last year had been: moving to Albuquerque, getting married, being deployed, and now Iraq. I wondered how many other married couples had spent their first year of marriage like this, together, in a war zone? It couldn't be that common. So many people had asked us things like, "How can you stand being in a war zone with your spouse? It's difficult enough being married, without the added stress." I suppose, from their point of view, it seemed strange. I couldn't imagine being here without Jake, and I knew he felt the same way.

"Hey, we should get something special for our anniversary," Jake mentioned, pointing out some strange-looking gold rings in the glass case. We must have been on the same wavelength, because I was looking at the same ones. The shop owner took a couple of them out, muttering something about the quality of the gold, but I didn't quite understand him. I had never been much for jewelry. However, this was our first anniversary, and it seemed inevitable that we would spend it in Iraq, and I thought, *Why not do something out of the ordinary?* We were on the longest, most bizarre honeymoon in history. Might as well indulge.

We were sitting on the shop steps, amusing each other by snapping the rings together and then pulling them apart, when SPC Johnson wandered over, took up a position leaning against the wall, and asked, "What are you guys doing for your leave?"

We hadn't thought we were getting leave—a couple months earlier, the scheduling detail had gone out and there hadn't been enough spaces for everyone to take time. Since we saw each other every day, we figured we could forfeit our time and let someone who really needed to see their family go home. "We don't have any," I said.

"Sure you do. With the extension, they have to give you leave," SPC Johnson said. "You've got, like, a whole two weeks coming to you."

Jake and I looked at each other. Two weeks away from the sandbox. We could do anything. We could go anywhere. We could take a real honeymoon, someplace that was actually *nice*.

CHAPTER 18

Überraschung

We'd been in Iraq for seven months, and in all that time, the weather had been a uniform teeth-melting 120 degrees. The sky was always a deep, boiling blue, and the only clouds we saw were made of dust. One morning, I stepped outside the tent and noticed that a couple other soldiers were looking up and pointing. I thought maybe they were looking at a plane or, God forbid, a missile, so I glanced up at the sky. There I saw a real, honest-to-goodness vapor cloud. Just a wispy little cirrus cloud, barely even there, but it was easily the most beautiful piece of weather I'd seen in months. Within a week, we'd gone from sweating twenty-four hours a day to digging our jackets out of the bottom of our duffle bags. It seemed like the temperature dropped fifty degrees overnight. I think we would have appreciated the difference more if it hadn't coincided with our leave.

Our leave began when we hitched an open-air ride on the back of a five-ton army truck for the three-hour drive to Camp Arifjan, everyone huddling close together to keep out of the wind and the cold. From there, we took a bus to Camp Doha, just outside Kuwait City. When we arrived at Doha we spoke to a military travel agent.

We fantasized about many different destinations: Hawaii, Italy, or Australia, discussing what we would do and the sights we would see. We really wanted to go to Hawaii, but when we did the math on how far we'd have to travel, we figured out that of our two weeks of leave, we'd end up with less than a week in paradise. We were literally on the other side of the planet, and getting there would entail at least three days of travel, each way, plus time changes. The travel agent suggested Germany. Apparently, there were some great military resorts scattered throughout the country. Who knew the army had resorts? We settled on Garmisch-Partenkirchen, a resort town in the mountains of Bavaria. The resort was run by the army, for the army, so we knew we'd be around other soldiers, and the staff would know what to expect from us. As a bonus, it was very affordable.

The travel agent had warned us that we would need to be in civilian clothes when we left the base for the airport. So we went to the PX, where we planned on stocking up on clothes for the trip. But once we started trying on clothes, we couldn't help but laugh at how ridiculous we looked. "Who the freak would buy this crap?"

"I don't know, but I'm pretty sure we'd stand out less in our uniforms."

The selection was terrible, and most of it didn't fit us, so we ended up buying a single outfit each. We didn't really care what the clothes looked like. As long as they weren't DCUs we were good. We just wanted to get going.

It wasn't until we were in the air that reality began to sink in. For the first time in months, we were making our own plans, following our own schedule, moving freely in a world where we neither had to follow orders nor look out for explosions. It felt strange, like a weight had been lifted, or a restraint released. Jake summed it up best, holding my hand as the airplane took flight: "It almost feels like we're breaking the rules."

Five hours later, we landed at the Frankfurt airport. We'd packed light—just a couple carry-on backpacks and ourselves—which turned out to be the right choice as it let us skip the baggage carousel and zip through the slow-moving airport crowds. Before we'd really thought about it, we'd gotten off the train in Frankfurt proper, and we were standing under the bright lights of a thriving metropolis, watching as fashionably dressed professionals ducked into the train station and out of the rain. I felt deeply out of place. Jake and I hadn't showered in two days, and our trashy PX clothes were nothing like what these urban Germans were sporting. We looked exactly like what we were: scruffy military personnel, unexpectedly on leave. We didn't even have hotel reservations.

We walked around the city for close to an hour until we found a trendy little place in a quiet part of town and secured a room. The room itself, while decidedly cute, was almost a caricature of European minimalism. It seemed like everything in it had been shrunk, or deliberately built for tiny people. Jake and I are not tall, so it was fine for us, but we couldn't imagine any hotel in the US actually expecting guests to stay in rooms built along these proportions. But none of that mattered. It was decorated in a modern, elegant style, and it beat the hell out of canvas tents and kangaroo rats.

"I'm going to take a shower," I said, as Jake slumped over on the bed. He murmured something into a pillow as I shucked off my terrible clothes. The shower was an elegant affair—wide, crystal clear plates of glass, a broad showerhead—and if you left the door to the bathroom open, it had a clear line of sight to the bed. I was stepping out of the shower when I noticed Jake ogling me. I smiled, gave him a little twirl. It was officially our one-year anniversary today of all days, after all, and in all that time, we'd never had a lot of completely private time together.

"Your boobs look amazing," Jake said as I sat down on the bed next to him, still toweling my hair dry. "It's like they've grown a couple sizes."

"What does *that* mean?" I asked, playfully letting my fingers tug off his shirt.

About an hour later, we were ready for dinner, though, to be honest, we might have been better off just staying in bed. Jet lag is no joke. We tried to make the night romantic, but as we pushed through the evening, we found ourselves trailing off at the sentence, completely losing the thread of a conversation.

Even so, we made it out onto the street, and into a restaurant that was so close to closing that the waitstaff shot us dirty looks as we came through the door. We sat and ate and tried to banter, but something was off. We were definitely tired, but it was more than that. We both had this weird feeling that we were missing something—a phantom need that made us antsy and quiet. The more we thought about it, the more menacing the people around us started to look. The dirty looks they'd given us when we first arrived seemed more pronounced. There was something deeply unsettling about how close they came to us. We paid the bill quickly and hustled back to our hotel, avoiding crowds, eager to escape that weird feeling we were both having. It was not the one-year anniversary dinner we had imagined.

The next day, we decided to ditch the grunts-on-leave look and go shopping for real clothes. I picked up a simple ivory-colored skirt, some ankle-high boots, and a suede coat that made me feel like we were positively made of money, while Jake found a respectable-looking button-down shirt and slacks, pairing them with a leather coat. We were the height of fashion, at least from our perspective.

Finally well-dressed and beginning to feel like real people again, we stepped back out into the street and conferred.

"What next?" I asked, pulling Jake out of the way of busy-looking Germans.

"I'm hungry," he said. "Let's find dinner."

When I was growing up, my family didn't take a lot of vacations. That is, we didn't do any overseas travel. Minnesota was about as exotic as we got. We went on plenty of road trips, and we saw plenty of the sights the US has to offer, but we never went somewhere just for the sake of relaxation. It was almost always to visit family. We were there to see someone, or for some holiday. This business of being in Germany just for the sake of being somewhere nice was kind of new to me. It seemed like a lot of it was just filling up the hours between meals.

"Okay," I said. "What do you want to eat?"

Jake grinned at me. He was in Germany, and his favorite type of food was German. "I was thinking schnitzel. And maybe some good beer?"

I blanched. "Oh, babe, can we maybe do that later?" Just the thought of it turned my stomach.

Jake's face fell. "But this is schnitzel-land. If you're ever going to have a good experience with German food, it's going to be in Germany."

"How about that place, over there?" I pointed at an Italian restaurant across the street. I knew where I stood with Italian food. Pasta was the same, no matter what country you ate it in.

But Jake just rolled his eyes. Those Chicagoan standards, up in arms again. "But we're in Germany," he said.

"Exactly! You can have German food anytime. Right now, though, I'm just tired, and I really want something familiar." I laid on the charm, good and thick. "Please, Jake?"

Jake sighed. "Okay," he said, and I mentally jumped for joy.

It was as we walked into the restaurant that we realized what that weird phantom need was: our knives and M16s were back in Iraq. Back on the pony express, we'd carried our weapons literally everyplace we went—from the trucks to the chow hall, we were never unprepared. But here we were, in civilization, sitting down to a truly exceptional meal, and we kept expecting to lean back against our chairs and feel the heft of our weapons. The feeling didn't leave us. After dinner, we walked around downtown—at one point wandering into the red-light district—and the feeling of vulnerability only grew. Have you ever had that dream where all of the sudden you realize you're walking around with no pants on? That's how we felt. We were unarmed, and vulnerable.

It was pretty clear that our feelings were unusual. Suited to the Iraqi desert, certainly, but not modern Germany. We knew that here, in this place, we would just have to second guess every emotion, every reactive thought. It meant that our vacation wasn't going to be all that relaxing, but considering how cautious our instincts were already, the chances that we'd have ever been able to relax were pretty low.

The next morning, we took the train from Frankfurt to Garmisch-Partenkirchen. A few hours into the ride, a German cop who wanted to see our IDs and go through our luggage approached us. Jake and I tried not to get upset—why would he single us out?—we knew he was just doing his job. It turned out that Americans traveling with minimal luggage are sometimes drug smugglers, or so the guy sitting behind us told us, so maybe he was right to check us out. As soon as he saw that we were just soldiers on leave, he handed back our IDs, shot us a disapproving look, and moved on.

If you haven't been to Germany, you've got to understand that apart from the sense of history that permeates every building, the countryside is breathtaking. It's everything I ever imagined the German countryside to be. Broad, rolling hills covered in lush, green grass—which, as we were coming from Iraq, was a radical difference—dotted with sheep, cows, and quaint old farms, all under a bright blue sky. The air itself was cool and crisp, scented with the promise of snow. I felt the generations of my German ancestors swelling with homesickness. I had a sudden impulse to grab a dirndl and dress Jake in some lederhosen.

Garmisch-Partenkirchen looked like the cover poster for every edition of the book *Heidi* I've ever seen. A town perched on the side of a mountain, the streets narrow and steep, flanked by ornately decorated buildings that wouldn't be out of place on a cuckoo clock. This was exactly what we were looking for. The quintessential German town, everything we'd ever imagined.

The resort, on the other hand, was a little piece of the US. There was a free meal service, an internet café, a game room, and hotel rooms that were obviously built with Americans in mind. American comforts surrounded by German scenery. The best of both worlds.

There was a lot to do, once we'd gotten ourselves situated. We took a trip to Neuschwanstein Castle, the inspiration for the castle in Disney's *Cinderella*, and we spent a day trying to go snowboarding in the Alps. Getting up the mountain and to the ski lodge involved a terrifyingly steep train ride, and reaching the slopes meant clinging to a guide rope like a helpless baby while our boards fishtailed beneath us, but at the end of the day, we got to curl up in a cozy ski lodge with a fire and some cocoa and laugh about it.

The morning after going snowboarding, I woke up nauseated. I hate being sick, so I tried to pretend I was fine, but violent vomiting put the kibosh on that plan. I went back to bed and hoped it would go away soon. Jake stood in the doorway of the bathroom for a moment, thinking, before crawling back into bed with me. "I don't want to freak you out," he said, which instantly did so. "But your boobs have gotten bigger. And now you're throwing up. I feel like maybe we should—"

"Shut up," I said, "that's not what's happening here."

"But maybe it is? We've been a little careless."

Careless. You put two married people in a stressful environment like a war zone, and they're going to have one or two lapses in judgement. They're going to take comfort in each other, regardless of the prophylactic situation. "Okay," I said, thinking about it. The times in the tent. The times in the Conex box. The times in the truck. "Maybe. We should get a test."

"Of course."

I got dressed and we headed out to procure a pregnancy test kit from the corner pharmacy. When we returned, I went straight to the bathroom. I peed on that stick like my life depended on it.

And then we waited.

An agonizing five minutes.

Time stood still. I swear, I was watching the clock, and it seemed like every click of the second hand took hours. I hadn't been this nervous since the first time I crossed into Iraq.

When the time was finally up, we went to compare the results to the instructions, only to discover that they were written entirely in German.

"What does it say?" I asked, squinting at the unfamiliar words. Pregnant? Not pregnant? My handbook of German phrases had not covered this possibility.

Jake just shook his head. "How should I know?"

"Your family is German," I said. "You love German food. Everything about your upbringing says you should know how to read this!"

"Well, I don't," he said, just as close to freaking out as I was. "Let's find someone who does."

"Who?"

He grabbed my hand and tugged me to my feet. "Front desk? Come on."

Together we grabbed an elevator. We must have made a strange sight: two American soldiers, holding hands in an elevator, one of them gingerly holding a home pregnancy test.

The lady at the front desk was young and smiled easily. I wondered how much training she'd had in dealing with distraught American soldiers, and if translating pregnancy tests was something she did all the time.

"Hi," Jake said, leaning against the counter and doing an impressive job of looking totally at ease. "We're sorry, but we wondered if you could translate something for us?"

"Of course," she said, in English that had only the slightest trace of a German accent.

We passed her the instructions, and then, somewhat more carefully, we held up the stick. She only had to glance at the test before grinning up at us. "Congratulations!" she said. "You're pregnant!"

I had to sit down.

I found an armchair with a view of the Alps, and was still for a moment, until Jake took a seat next to me. "You okay?" he asked.

"I think so. Maybe."

"We always said that we wanted kids."

"Yeah. I know, it's just I want them a year or two from now."

"Yeah, that would be preferable, but we are kinda committed here."

We're always on the same page. "It's just . . . I don't want to leave you."

That was the problem. Not the baby. If I was going to be pregnant, the military wasn't about to let me stay in Iraq (not that I wanted to be there, either. Just the thought of dodging bullets while pregnant made me queasier than I'd been before). They'd ship me home as soon as they knew. Jake would have to stay, though. He'd have to be there for the rest of his tour, and be there without me watching his back. I mean, obviously, he can take care of himself, but this is what marriage is. You're supposed to support each other. Separating meant that neither of us would be able to do that.

That evening, as soon as the time difference meant we wouldn't be waking anyone up, we called our families to break the news. My family and friends were ecstatic. My parents were beyond thrilled that I'd be coming home. Jake's family took it differently—they were a bit more pragmatic. Jake's sister thought it was weird that we'd try to start a family while we were overseas. Jake tried to explain without really explaining, but the concept just seemed like foreign territory to her.

It was strange, but just learning about my pregnancy made the morning sickness worse. And I developed a bunch of food aversions—especially to German food. Poor Jake just couldn't catch a break. He suffered through my quest to eat only terrible American junk food—Pizza Hut and Subway—while real, authentic German food and beer tantalized him from every street corner.

As our time in Germany drew to a close, we became much more aware of how little time we had left together. Every day, it got harder to face. Back at the Frankfurt airport, we bought matching watches so I could always know the time in Iraq. We were sitting on a bench, synchronizing the times, when the first wave of grief washed over me. I was going to have to leave my best friend, my lover, my everything. The man who was my home. I broke into ragged sobs, and Jake held me while I wept.

When we got back to Camp Arifjan, we told the warrant officer who was in charge of our unit's behind-the-lines operations. He wasn't terribly surprised—we are a married couple, after all—but said we had to go through official channels, get the blood test and everything, before he could set up the paperwork. We could have stalled—maybe tried to drag out our time together—but this strange sense of purpose had gripped me. If I couldn't have Jake's back in battle, I had to put that same protective energy into keeping this baby safe. And no baby was safe in a war zone.

The blood test came back positive, and I was told that I had a few days to get ready before I shipped out. I made the most of those days, despite the fact that every time I smelled diesel, I had to throw up. There was a diesel generator right next to the chow hall, so every time we entered the chow trailer, I'd have to throw up first. There were definitely things about this place that I wasn't going to miss.

For those last few days, I stuck to Jake like glue. We didn't let anything separate us. We knew that the future was full of hazards—Jake was going to continue fighting this war, but he'd have to do it without me, and I had all new battles to fight, first with my body, to make sure it safely grew a baby, and then with the civilian world, which I knew was going to feel strange and alien. We spent those last few days wandering around Camp Arifjan, talking about what our new life would be like once we were back together. We talked about what being parents would be like, and what we wanted to do with our lives beyond the war. Faced with the sudden knowledge that he was going to have to take care of a family, of a little person who genuinely *couldn't* take care of himself or herself, Jake decided that he was going to have to go back to school and finally finish the degree he'd started.

At some point during our wanderings, we found ourselves in the PX, looking at the sweetest Winnie the Pooh blanket. We knew instantly that it was going to be one of our baby's first blankets. That it came from the Middle East made it meaningful—it would follow our child's journey and be with him or her from the beginning.

As the last day dawned, Jake and I stayed in our cots a few moments longer. "I don't know how I'll cope without you," Jake said, pulling me closer. I buried my head in his chest. We were best friends. Battle buddies. We were everything to each other.

"I know how strong you are," I told him. "You're going to survive this place, and you're going to come home to me. To us."

But that was the morning.

When it finally came to it, standing in front of the car, ready to start the trip to the airport, I couldn't say goodbye. Jake was strong and stoic for the both of us, but I was a wreck.

I clung to him long after I was supposed to get into the car, my eyes streaming, my sobbing uncontrollable. How could I leave? How could I do this without him? Finally, he pushed me into the car, and I watched through the window as his figure grew smaller in the distance. Of all the hard things that we had been through together—the ambushes, the anxiety, the heat, the bugs—this was by far the hardest. To this day, it makes both of us well up in tears.

CHAPTER 19

Homecoming

I had to get my discharge papers from El Paso, which was a dozen different kinds of miserable. All of the people I had known there were back in Iraq, so I spent the time simultaneously lonely, surrounded by strangers, missing my husband, and basically struggling to fit back into the non-war-zone mentality world. Spending every night inside a building with a roof over my head felt foreign. I had a strange urge to grab my sleeping bag and sleep under the stars. The army had recently set up call-center tents in most of the camps, so Jake could call me once a week or so. Just the thought of hearing his voice helped me push through to the next week, until I could talk to him again. I wished that I could reach through the phone and drag him back to me.

The longer I stayed in El Paso, the more clearly I understood that there was no way in hell I was going back to live in

Albuquerque. Being alone and pregnant on a base was awful enough. I couldn't imagine how terrible it would be to be alone in the civilian world, with no support system at all. I had to move back home with my parents, even if the idea made me a little crazy.

My dad met me in the Albuquerque airport, standing at the bottom of the arrivals escalator as I slowly descended. Seeing him for the first time in close to a year—my dad, the man I'd looked for in every man until I met Jake, the man who showed me how strength and kindness have always been the same thing—made my heart thrum. As he came into view, I thought about how much had changed—I'd barely been married when I last saw him, and now I was a combat veteran, and pregnant with his grandchild. He couldn't have known that he'd ever see me again. I saw him tear up as I rushed into his arms.

He was there to help me drive my car back to Iowa. The motor was dead—a year in storage had done it no favors—but we got a mechanic to come out and start it, and then we set off. It was good to be back with my dad, and over the course of the road trip, I felt like we were getting to know one another all over again. It wasn't like much had changed for him, but I felt different. It had been just a couple years since college, when I'd been able to run home whenever I wanted to, but to me, it felt like decades. I'd traveled the world and fallen in love. I'd lived through a war, and now my body was building a baby. I don't know that he necessarily had the tools to understand how much I had changed, but he was prepared to be there for me—to love me like he always had—no matter who I turned out to be.

232

Eagle Grove was also unchanged. Sure, there were yellow ribbons on the trees outside my parents' houses, and it was nearly Christmas, so the town looked appropriately festive, but it was all the same seasonal changes that made up the old, familiar rhythm of the town. Nothing new. In the last two years, I'd gone from town to town, and then from country to country, constantly confronted with new sights and new ways of doing things. Back in Eagle Grove, I'd have to get used to being the only thing that changed.

It made me restless. I kept looking for something. It was a week or two before I realized that every time I went around a corner, I was secretly expecting Jake to be there, waiting for me. I so wanted him to be there, and every time, he wasn't. I comforted myself by saying it wouldn't be long, just a few short months, until he was safely home with me. I tried to pretend that the time wasn't crawling by.

Adjusting to civilian life was its own challenge. I didn't notice it at first. It didn't hit me until I'd been home for a month or so. I was alternating weeks with each set of parents, spending the days in their living rooms while everybody else went to work, alone with my thoughts. Snow outside. Limited daylight. I'd stare out the window for hours, thinking about Jake, stuck in Iraq, the pulse of his weeks marked by missions and battle.

A few months into my pregnancy, depression merged with anxiety, and I started having panic attacks. PTSD combined with my out-of-whack hormones left me crying all the time. I was a wreck. My mom was the first to understand what was happening. She was the one who helped me through that first panic attack, shepherding me to a quiet place with simple soothing phrases: "You're safe. You're okay. I love you." I don't know what would have happened if she hadn't been there. But there's a difference between getting me through one attack and getting me through a future of PTSD. My parents did everything they could to help me, but they weren't equipped to deal with this level of emotional aftershock. I quickly realized that I needed professional help.

A doctor at the VA facility in Des Moines gave me a prescription for antidepressants. Jake objected when we talked on the phone—he worried about what the drugs would do to our baby—but I knew that the baby wouldn't be healthy unless I was. And, to be fair, I wouldn't have taken the prescription if my OB hadn't okayed it. It was hard for Jake to understand what I was going through. Just a few short weeks ago we were both battling insurgents on the highways of Iraq. Now we were worlds apart, both literally and figuratively. My mission was to ensure that we had a healthy baby, and his was to come home.

Jake called me as often as possible, or whenever he got back from a mission—I knew that his worries were less about the medical situation and more about our separation. There was a part of him that thought my depression was entirely the result of the distance between us—that if he was home with me, I wouldn't have gotten sick.

But the truth is that PTSD isn't something you can fix just by having your husband around. War changes you. When you come back, you see that all the complaints you ever had about your life were laughably trivial. You look around and see nonsoldiers with those same complaints, and you can't imagine how they can be so blind. Don't they see how great their lives are? They have peace and pleasure and ease, and they're complaining about a little traffic? They have no idea how bad life can get. Seeing the way so many Americans take our homeland for granted brought to the surface an intense patriotism I hadn't fully appreciated. Sometimes you don't know how valuable something is until you've seen people without it. When I first took the oath of enlistment, it sent chills down my spine. Now, knowing fully what I would do to protect my country, that memory is tied up with even more meaning and emotion. My time overseas revealed a devotion to my country, a sense of patriotism, which will always run through my blood.

While I was in Iraq, I looked for the good in any moment. The moments that I could laugh about, or the moments when I felt like I'd made a friend or bonded with someone new, or even just learned about a perspective I'd never considered. I'd put a lot of effort into finding ways to stay positive, to avoid focusing on the misery, paranoia, and violence I experienced every day. I'd built up a mental shield, designed to keep the person I was—underneath all of that danger—safe. And that shield wasn't going to go away anytime soon.

In fact, when I got home, that shield went on the offensive. It mistook innocuous things for dangers, and turned the reflexive responses I'd developed overseas into panic over nothing. I couldn't stand to be around large groups of people because something in the back of my mind worried that one of them was planning to shoot me. Every time I saw trash by the side of the road, I was sure it was a bomb. Every time we drove under an overpass, I was sure that the people above us were going to attack. But here was the kicker: I knew that these responses were irrational on some level, but in the moment, it's hard to know what's real. I knew that I was safe. But that little voice in the back of my mind, telling me to look for every possible danger, never really went away.

This isn't a perspective that wins many friends. Before going overseas, I'd loved going out with my friends, but when I got home, I couldn't relate to anyone. It sounds terrible, but it took a lot of effort to act like I cared about their problems. It was really tiring. A simple conversation with a stranger was enough to send me back to bed for the afternoon.

I missed the days in Iraq when I knew the importance of every moment. Sure, we'd spent a fair amount of time napping in the trucks and bitching about the food, but we always knew that our time there had a purpose. Back at home, I was just sitting around, gestating. I was miserable.

I can't imagine what PTSD must be like for soldiers who get home and don't have a family to build. The hardest thing for me to adjust to was the idea that my days didn't necessarily have a mission associated with them, that I could just do whatever and it wouldn't matter. In Iraq, no matter how horrifying it had gotten, I'd always known what my purpose was. If I hadn't been pregnant when I got home, I wouldn't have known what to do with myself. Knowing that I was in charge of this little life, that I was responsible for making it the best it could be, was the only thing that gave my life direction.

It didn't help that I kept having nightmares. Deeply vivid, horrifying nightmares of the people I loved being injured or killed in combat. Violent image after violent image. I barely slept, and when I did, I got no comfort from it. Considering my sleep was so bad, it was no surprise that I kept mistaking ordinary aspects of civilian life for mortal dangers. My brain was simply not functioning at 100 percent.

The meds helped, finally. I still missed Jake, and I still beat myself up over leaving before completing the job, but the meds gave my brain time to breathe. They let me function. The panic attacks grew less frequent, the horrible thoughts receded, and the nightmares got milder. It felt miraculous. Not to downplay the problem: I knew that my PTSD wasn't cured. Medication doesn't fix everything itself—therapy is essential—and the road to a healthy mind is long. Heck, it's been thirteen years and I'm still working through it.

As I started to get better, the weather grew warmer. Springtime in Iowa is always an epiphany. One day you're bundled up, cracking the ice in puddles on the road, and the next day, the trees are budding and the daffodils are blooming. I started going on a lot of walks. Partly because natural beauty is tremendously soothing, and partly because my body was changing. I was curvier than I'd ever been before, and I didn't want my size to limit me.

Day after day—meds, walking, thinking. My belly kept growing, and with each doctor's visit, I was reminded that time was passing, and soon Jake would be home with me.

At least, I hoped he would be home soon. When we'd first received our orders, our tour was for a flat six months. At the end of those six months, we were given new orders for 365 days and a promise that the tour wouldn't be extended again. It was now the end of February 2004, and at every call from Jake I expected to hear some news about his return. But sometimes, no news is good news.

"Hello?" I waited for the strange pause to pass and knew it was Jake. We always ended each call with a plan for when he would try to call again.

"Hey honey, how are you feeling?"

"Just fine," I said. "Any news about when you're coming home?" We had been apart for almost four months now, and I missed him so much it hurt.

"Yeah, well I got some news . . ."

Jake proceeded to tell me that he had new orders, and this time they were open-ended. The army wasn't even trying to give us false hopes about an eventual return date. I was pissed. How long could they keep a unit there? A year? Two years? Maybe Jake was right, and we should start looking at real estate in Kuwait (although Baghdad was more in our budget).

I couldn't bear the idea that Jake might not get home in time for the baby, so I chose to ignore it. I focused on the things I could do something about: my health, the health of my baby, and my relationship with my in-laws.

I hadn't spent much time with them, but Jake's parents were looking forward to his return just as much as I was. Jake's mom even invited me out to Chicago for a baby shower. I was a little leery at first—as far as I knew, their perception of me wasn't exactly complimentary—but I went. It was time for us all to really get to know each other.

Jake's father was a fireman/paramedic, and every time he got behind the wheel he drove as though it were an ambulance.

It was terrifying. I kept thinking, "I made it through months of battle in Iraq, but this is how I'm going to die." My mother-in-law recommended that I just close my eyes and pretend it wasn't happening, but I didn't really feel like that was an option. Once you know something, you can't unknow it. I white-knuckled the whole trip to the house, but we got there in once piece, and were promptly rewarded with the sight of Cody and Barley, the dogs Jake and I had had a lifetime ago. I couldn't believe that they remembered me. They jumped on me as soon as I was out of the car.

I spent a week in Chicago with my in-laws, and actually had a really good time. I got to know Jake's parents and siblings. My mother-in-law took me shopping in a high-end maternity store and bought me a ridiculously expensive dress to wear to pick up Jake at the airport. The baby shower was a success. I met dozens of Jake's family and friends, including his grandmother—who, it turned out, was a bit of a pistol! She and I hit it off right away, and by the time I had to leave, I was already thinking of her as my own grandma.

Back in Iowa, I had a second baby shower to attend, which I was sharing with Tiffany, who was due a month before me. Her mom, my mom, and my stepmom were hosting this one, and it seemed like everyone from our church was coming. They loaded us up with baby supplies, and I couldn't have been more grateful. I felt so loved and so cared for. I know I've said a lot about the importance of moving away from home and having adventures, but the reality is that when you're trying to build a family, you need as much support as you can get. Having a home in the community that raised you is like winning the support lottery. Everything I needed was built into the fabric of my hometown. Regardless of the PTSD, Jake's absence, or the strains of carrying a child, I felt inexpressibly blessed.

Jake came home on a two-week leave a week or so before my due date (which was July 4th, if you can believe it). I met him at the airport in Des Moines, wearing the maternity sundress his mom had bought me, freaking out because I was huge and he'd only ever seen me as a skinny, little waif. We had balloons and a giant "welcome home" banner, and as every person walked through the arrivals gate, my heart jumped in my chest. Was that him? No. How about him? No.

I got a glimpse of a shaved head, and I instantly recognized him. The pressure grew in my head and I felt my heart swell with joy. I was so overwhelmed that I burst into tears and ran to him. He dropped his bags and got his arms free just in time for me to tackle him. Eight long months of separation, and now I was in his arms once more. When I had stopped sobbing, and his own tears had slowed, he pushed me away to look at me properly. Smeared makeup, a belly the size of a beach ball, and still, his first words to me were, "You are more beautiful than ever."

I buried my head in his chest and swore to duct-tape us together. He laughed, and held me. We stood there for so long that the arrivals traffic got a little backed up.

We spent the next few days decompressing with my parents. I was too big to do much adventuring, so we mostly sat inside and talked. Jake found civilian life just as strange as I had. Even with my meds and therapy, there's no real comparison to just talking to someone else who understands. The longer we spent together, the more we felt like we were building each other up. Getting each other ready for whatever came next.

And what came next, came early. On June 23, 2004, a few days after Jake's arrival, I got hit with contractions. We knew that sometimes women experience phantom contractions before the baby is ready to come, but my mom sent us to the hospital early anyway. It was a good thing she did.

We got to the hospital and the nurses were great about quickly checking me and hooking me up to the monitor so they could keep track of my contractions. I had decided against pain meds, and they were pretty much respectful of that decision. My contractions weren't progressing very rapidly, so my doctor started me on a very small amount of Pitocin, which worked alarmingly well. My contractions sped up, got more painful, and had me working so hard that the sweat was pouring off me. I was convinced that someone had mistakenly turned on the heating instead of the air conditioning, so as the nurses adjusted the thermostat to be colder, and then colder again, poor Jake sat next to me (still acclimated to the heat of Iraq), bundled up against the cold, trying to feed me ice chips.

I labored all day and night, but as 3:00 a.m. approached, my doctor explained that our baby's head was too big for me. I'd never wanted a C-section, but it had become clear that there was no alternative.

I was awake for the surgery, but blissfully anesthetized, with a curtain hiding the surgeon's activity from me. But Jake watched the surgery. He said it was like something out of a horror movie—watching the doctors pull out my organs, hose them down, and then stuff them back inside—all while I was cracking jokes and telling stories. And before I knew it, I felt a little tug, and our baby had come into the world.

A boy.

We named him Wyatt, which means "Little Warrior."

If he'd been a girl, we would have called her "Summer." We'd chosen these names back in Germany, when we first learned that we were expecting. We'd gone back to the hotel room and talked for hours about what kind of parents we wanted to be, and what lessons we wanted to instill in our children.

And we'd talked about names.

We both loved the name Wyatt, though neither of us knew what it meant. Later, after I'd come home, I spent a little time leafing through a baby name book, and that was when I learned the meaning of his name. That was also when I realized that I *knew* we would have a little boy. It was too perfect that the name we'd chosen, just because we'd liked the sound of it, would be so appropriate to the circumstances of his conception. I knew that he had to be a boy. I knew it deep down in my soul. I knew it so thoroughly that when the doctor pulled him out and said, "It's a boy," I said to myself, "Well, obviously. I knew that already."

He had a ring around his head from trying to push through my uncooperative pelvis, and he was perfect in every way.

I wasn't that enthusiastic when the whole family descended on my hospital room, everyone crowding around, eager to see the baby. But you cope. I knew that when I'd slept and eaten and let all the crazy birth hormones subside, I'd be grateful for their presence. But right at that moment, all I wanted was to hold my baby and rest my head on Jake's chest. Eventually, after hugs, smiles, and the odd personally invasive question, the family departed and left us in peace. The nurses made us an adorable candlelit dinner, just for the two of us, and we breathed a heavy sigh of relief. It had turned out okay. We were turning out okay.

Jake, Wyatt, and I were lying outside looking up at the stars on a hot June evening a few days after I was let out of the hospital. Wyatt wasn't really looking but cuddled up napping between us, on the blanket. We were enjoying a brief moment of silence and stillness. It brought me back to our nights in Camp Cedar, falling asleep while gazing up at the twinkling night sky, and to my childhood, sitting right out here with my sister. It reminded me of that conversation so many years ago, and how at the time, I had pictured her as the friend who would join me in exploring the world. I still treasure the relationship with my sister, but I managed to find something that I could never have imagined as a seven-year-old.

Jake leaned over, carefully trying not to wake Wyatt up. "You know I have to go back tomorrow."

I knew, but at least we had the night.

Homemaking

When Jake's tour finally ended a few months later, he wanted to work full-time while finishing his BA—none of which would have been possible if we'd stayed in Iowa. Since I was staying home with Wyatt, the only way we could reasonably make our plan happen was if we moved in with his parents. They set us up in Jake's sister's old bedroom, and while I'm not going to say that it wasn't a squeeze, together we made it work. It was a little reminiscent of our early days in Iraq, as we were now spending our nights wrapped around each other on a tiny twin bed. Living so close to his family made us all crazy (his dad was a Vietnam vet, so there were three people dealing with PTSD under one roof), but after a few months, Jake and I helped his parents remodel their basement into a cute little apartment, and everything got easier.

Jake found a job that would keep us afloat while he went to school, and I started working on my personal training certification. This was one of the hidden benefits of moving in with your in-laws—for a whole six months, Jake's mom was willing to look after Wyatt in the afternoons while I pursued the only career that perfectly fit my personality and interests. Becoming a personal trainer was the next natural step for me, but I'd needed time and reflection to figure it out. I was so grateful that Jake's mom was willing to help me pursue it as a career.

About nine months after Wyatt was born, we learned that we were expecting a second child. Jake's parents worried that this new pregnancy would derail our educational and career goals, but eventually they came around. It's impossible to resist the allure of a new grandchild. And the truth is that Jake and I made an excellent team. We had goals, and we were working to achieve them. Not even a new baby was going to stand in the way.

One of those goals was to find a place of our own. Jake's parents owned the house across the street, and, with a second baby coming, it just seemed easier for us to move in and have our own space. We couldn't buy it from them, so we rented, which made us all happy—Jake didn't feel beholden to them anymore, and his parents felt like they were being supportive of us while still encouraging our independence.

I finished my certification and started taking clients, leaving Wyatt with a family friend while I went to work at the gym. I loved going to work. I've always loved working, but this was work that appealed to my passions, and I got to work with kind, laid-back people who shared my goals and interests. It was perfect for me.

Wyatt grew fat and happy, with a sweet, affectionate personality and a delight in cars and trains and Legos, just like his dad. And I kept getting bigger. The bigger I got, the more I just wanted to stay home with Wyatt. I loved my personal trainer gig, but the pull of taking care of my kids was too strong to keep it up. We also figured out that the cost of having two kids in day care was more than I earned as a trainer, so it just didn't make sense to keep doing it. Besides, I wanted to be home with my babies. I wanted to be there for every minute of their childhood.

My entire time growing up, I never thought I would be a stay-at-home-mom. I had a strong work ethic, and never understood why someone would choose to do that. Glamour was never my thing, and I'd always found jobs and activities that were traditionally more masculine. Most of my girlfriends found jobs as waitresses or cashiers. I choose to load heavy packages into trucks. While they spent time shopping, I would be baiting hooks and catching fish. I was one of the few girls in my town who joined the military, and the only one who decided to be a truck driver. So, I surprised myself when I decided to do this, to be the stay-at-home-mom. Maybe it was partially because I had had the chance to do all these things that I was so sure about my decision. I knew that I could do anything that I set my mind to, and I knew the most important job in the world was raising my children.

Our second child arrived at five in the morning, just like Wyatt had. My hips cooperated this time, so she was born in the usual way, kicking and screaming her way into our lives. Our little girl, our baby Summer. She was beautiful. In a weird coincidence, she shared the same birth statistics as her brother: both of them clocking in at seven pounds, nineteen inches.

With two kids, our home life kicked into overdrive. We bought a minivan, and I embraced my new soccer-mom identity. Trips to the library, play dates, time at the park—I made it all happen. They're not kidding when they say that being a mom is a full-time job. Jake's load was even heavier, as he divided his time between putting in a full day's work and then studying every night. It wasn't an easy path, not for either of us, but together, we did it.

Money was always a problem, as was finding intimate time together. Paying the bills was a two-person job, with Jake making the money and me making sure we got the most out of every dollar. That was an achievement by itself, but combined with the other stressors in our lives, it felt monumental. Keeping our sex life healthy was a different challenge. What with the kids and Jake's workload, combined with depression, PTSD, and the side effects of the meds we needed to manage those conditions, at the end of the day, we were both exhausted, and neither Jake nor I felt all that enthusiastic about getting close.

Without sex, a marriage is going to struggle. When one partner pulls away, the other feels unloved, and pulls away even further, perpetuating a cycle that can result in a permanent separation. I'm not saying that everyone wants the same thing from his or her partner, but people in a marriage undisputedly need each other, both physically and emotionally. Every relationship requires effort from both parties. And every relationship requires communication. Without communication, everything falls apart. It took some time for Jake and me to figure that out but when we finally did, our relationship grew stronger every day. We still work on it.

Jake finished his master's degree at around the time Wyatt started preschool. We were all so incredibly proud of him. He'd worked so hard for so long, and now he was ready to reap the rewards. It goes to show, when you put your mind to something and focus on any goal, hard work and perseverance pay off. He quickly found a great software developing job. It paid well, had great benefits, and was close to home. The years leading up to this achievement had been exhausting for all of us, but it had all been worth it. We'd known what we were working toward, and we'd worked together to make it a success.

Jake's new job changed everything for us. It gave us stability and security, and it let us save up and finally build our own dream home. We found a new subdivision with a brand-new elementary school, and we bought enough property for a new house and a bit of acreage for a yard. We even got to personalize the design of the house.

Back when we were living in the little house across the street from Jake's parents, Jake had made me a promise: "Heidi, I promise you that within the next few years, we will be making enough money, and we will buy a house together." And it happened. It happened because we believed in each other and we were there for one another. Jake is the hardest-working man I know, and he keeps moving up in the world. Together, we keep making life better for our family. Marriage is teamwork and we have to be there to help each other succeed. Jake never fails to tell me that none of his achievements would have been possible without my support. By the same token, none of the things I've achieved would have been possible without his support. We are always there for one another, no matter what happens.

Dream big and go after that dream with all you've got. We live in the greatest country on the planet, where everyone has the freedom to either succeed or fail. It is up to you to decide if you want your life to be successful.

From the moment Jake and I met, we knew we would be together forever. Our life together has been anything but easy, but our triumphs have far outpaced our trials. Never give up on life or marriage. There's always a way through, you just have to keep faith, keep working, and keep looking for the good things. You can find those bright patches of sunlight in every situation; it just takes a little dogged determination. I could not have asked for a better partner. We've learned a lot in the short fifteen years we've been married, and we know that we still have a lot to learn. The most important thing we've learned is that so long as we stick together and keep our lines of communication open, our bond will keep getting stronger.

It's all worth it. I promise.

If you enjoyed this book and would like
to reach out to the author, please contact her
at heidi@radpublished.com.

Made in the USA
Columbia, SC
28 February 2021